REVIVAL RISING

REVIVAL RISING

EMBRACING HIS TRANSFORMING FIRE

KIM MEEDER

Chosen
a division of Baker Publishing Group
Minneapolis, Minnesota

Published by Chosen Books
11400 Hampshire Avenue South
Bloomington, Minnesota 55438
www.chosenbooks.com

Chosen Books is a division of
Baker Publishing Group, Grand Rapids, Michigan

Printed in the United States of America

ISBN 978-0-8007-9953-3

Library of Congress Cataloging-in-Publication Control Number: 2019057455

In some of the author's stories, the names and identifying details of certain individuals have been changed to protect their privacy.

Cover design by Darren Welch Design

20   21   22   23   24   25   26   7   6   5   4   3   2   1

This book is dedicated to love—
love for the Father, Son and Holy Spirit—
and to those who choose to embrace,
be filled by and release His love
with all their heart, soul, mind
and strength.

Contents

Foreword

Kim Meeder is a gifted storyteller who has an incredible passion for pointing people toward the healing power of Christ. I have been privileged to welcome her as a guest on the *Focus on the Family Broadcast* several times, and she never fails to bring uplifting words of hope and encouragement.

Kim's love for those who bear deep emotional wounds is especially evident in her ongoing work with children at the Crystal Peaks Youth Ranch. I can relate to some of those kids because as a child, I was shaken and torn. I have experienced what it is like to feel lost, adrift and disconnected from anything resembling stability and wholeness. Kim's heart is to help those precious kids understand their identity in Christ. It is impossible to overstate just how important that is!

As you will discover in the pages of this book, Kim has a unique awareness of God's presence and the movement of His Spirit in the everyday moments of life. This acuity reminds me of the words of David when he wrote, "Where shall I go from your Spirit? Or where shall I flee from your presence?" (Psalm 139:7 ESV).

Kim understands that we cannot hide from God. He knows us and He is with us *always*, even in the darkest of moments when we feel as if He is far away. His hand is evident in every situation if we will just take time to look for it, and that is what Kim so brilliantly captures.

God is with you. He loves you. His Spirit surrounds you, indwells you and nourishes you. These are themes that are repeated over and over throughout the pages of *Revival Rising*. I am thankful that Kim has shared this faith-affirming and spiritually enriching message with her readers. It is something we all need to hear!

Jim Daly
President, Focus on the Family

Preface

I love the wilderness places in this world, because this is where I hear the voice of my God most clearly. For this wild heart, the higher I go, driven by my unique DNA to seek the solace of the mountains, the closer my heart feels to His. And within these lofty places, the noise of humanity is silenced by the raw, unshakable power of the presence of God.

Because I live on the eastern slope of the Cascade Mountain range in the Pacific Northwest, I have a spectacular selection of stand-alone volcanos in my front yard. Recently, I enjoyed an amazing day climbing the South Sister. About one thousand feet below the 10,358-foot summit is one of my all-time favorite mountain features. If you are not looking up, it would be easy to miss this rock wall, not uncommon in the high elevations. But what makes this wall unusual is how it has been cut so sharply that its highest reaches literally curve backward into midair like leftover ice cream. It resembles a massive ocean wave of stone, three stories high, curling into the endless blue of the Central Oregon sky.

What could sever a vertical wall of rock with such supreme force, with such titanic impact? What moves with ease . . . the immovable?

Unfathomable light shines, radiant with power, glory and peace in the presence of absolute love. Unstoppable waves of reverberating worship encircle the throne of God like harmonic echoes of sheer gold. Beauty covers all. Authority permeates all. Love fills all. Caught up in the wonder is a single perfect snowflake—a tiny masterpiece created in the glory of heaven. Formed around a fragment of dust, it is unique and beautiful, a stunning singular design that hovers in the presence of God.

Then, a voice thunders from the throne, "My beloved, it is time." The snowflake's focus changes from overwhelming awe to utter confusion.

The voice of the One clarifies, "It is time to leap forward into My perfect plan. It is time to fly into the realm for which you were created. I am sending you out into the blackness. I am sending you to earth . . . to transform it for My glory."

Without words, the snowflake's gaze moves from outward to inward. *Who am I? I'm only one. I have no weight, no authority, no power to change anything. My magnificent exterior was designed around a fragment of dust. Dust! My very core is dirt. And yet, God . . . You would choose me? Why would You send me? Father, this makes no sense. Why must I leave the beauty, comfort and glory of Your presence?*

Again, His loving voice resounds. "Because My will cannot be carried out on earth as it is in heaven . . . if you chose to stay in heaven. For the world to be transformed by My glory, my glorious ones need to go!"

With understanding, resolve and trust, the snowflake concedes, *I'm created by You, beloved by You and now charged by You to move forward into the greater purpose for which I was designed. I don't need to understand my outcome to choose Your will over mine. I will leave heaven's glory and go into any darkness You command. I love You more. More than my comfort. More than my will. More than me.*

Here I am, God. You can send me.

God's voice thunders, "Go! Go, My beloved, into all the world!" The single snowflake nods, then leaps into the unknown.

Alone it falls, twists, glides, deeper and deeper into black upon black. Heaven's glory fades as the gloom of earth looms closer. Falling into utter darkness, the solitary snowflake rolls over to take one last look at the glory from which it came . . . and is astonished by what it sees.

It is not alone.

Other snowflakes are emerging through the dusk. The dark sky transforms with their glorious presence. Millions upon millions of others are coming, too.

A great blizzard of glory swirls down through the night. Form to form, they combine. Glory to glory. Purity upon purity, white upon white, they gather. Soon they are no longer singular but compress into a formidable force. Their numbers reach beyond comprehension.

Bound by the power of God Himself, they become a mighty glacier. Their combined willingness and uniqueness become a force that obliterates stone, even the rock of a mountain, as they usher in an unstoppable presence, *His* presence, on earth.

A lone snowflake is unique, glorious, beautiful, but can be destroyed with a single breath. Yet when they gather and conjoin, there is nothing in the realm of men that can stop them.

Friend, we are like that: specifically designed by the Father for a unique purpose. And in the same way, our Creator is calling you, *My beloved, it is time.*

On this day, what will you choose? Your will . . . or His?

Each of us must choose within our own heart: revival's sudden death . . . or sudden ignition.

The sudden death of revival is fueled by our complacent, prideful self-justification. The sudden ignition of revival is fueled by our love so great for Him that we do not desire anything other than His will.

Complacency or ignition? Prideful self-justification or love for the Father? No one else is responsible to choose for you . . . but you.

No snowflake can choose to go for another. And in this way, every blizzard starts the same: with one single beautiful flake driven by pure love for the One who made it. And this choice, combined with the saints before, is what carves through hearts of stone like a knife through ice cream.

This is what moves the immovable—with ease. This is the power, the titanic impact, of our Father's love.

Introduction

Genuine revival is born out of genuine love for God. Because of love, Jesus entered earth's atmosphere to break the power of sin and death and to set the captives free. He showed us step for step how to love others to life—with His own life. He is not asking us; He is commanding us to do the same.

Revival is not something that happens *around* us. It is something that happens *in* us.

As believers, we have been commanded to fulfill what Jesus started. He has fully equipped us with His name, His blood, His Word, His giftings and His Spirit. Yet most of us remain largely inactive, stalled out, somehow feeling ill-equipped for the task of carrying His redemption forward.

Friend, the world around you is dying without hope. Family, friends and co-workers are collapsing in the darkness of sin and suffering. Jesus' commissioning, His command over your life has not changed. He is calling you—*you*—to carry the living flame that is Him into the blackness and deliver the blaze of His life-giving love.

Revival rises when one heart after another is set on fire with the unquenchable inferno of His loving freedom.

It is not forged out of what we do. Rather, authentic revival begins as the overflow of a heart and life so filled with gratitude and love for Jesus that His presence pours out into the world around us in a natural way. It is the unstoppable ignition of His love flowing within us that becomes the Great Commission flowing out through us.

Revival will rise when we let go of all other things—and choose His love to become the fuel that drives us to embrace His transforming fire.

Today, Jesus, ignite all that I am—heart, soul, mind, strength—to burn for only You.

The world around me will not change—until I do. The transformation I seek begins with me. When I am fully consumed in the flame of Your presence, this is where revival will rise from my life.

Jesus, I ask for Your true redemption over my human religion. I release my humanity and ask for Your humility. I submit to the inferno of Your transforming love to fill all that I am. Only then will the atmosphere around me be revived by the heat of Your redeeming passion through me.

May Your presence beam through me and raise a revival in my nation, my state, my county, my city, my neighborhood, my family and my home.

Your Word promises, "If my people who are called by my name will humble themselves and pray and seek my face and turn from their wicked ways, I will hear from heaven and will forgive their sins and restore their land" (2 Chronicles 7:14).

The ignition of my revival begins with bowing before You in humility, prayer, seeking, turning.

If I, this vessel, will persist in these four weapons of revival, then You will hear, forgive and heal the land of my heart, home and country.

I place my heart to be deeply united with Your heart in humility. I position my soul to be in constant communion with Your soul through prayer. I yield my mind to being pliable before Your mind and turn where You desire. I pursue with all the strength that is within me to seek You above all else.

Upon this bedrock, I submit myself in Your presence to be saturated with Your merciful healing—and forgiveness. From this foundation, I can be filled up and poured out for Your glory.

May I understand the power of Your complete redemption and wholeness working to create in me a unique weapon of loving warfare, ready to carry the light of my God into the darkness.

Today I commit with all that I am to embrace the transforming fire that is Your presence.

Let Your revival rise in me.

REAWAKEN MY HEART

Jesus replied, "The most important commandment is this: 'Listen, O Israel! The LORD our God is the one and only LORD. And you must love the LORD your God with all your *heart . . .*'"

Mark 12:29–30, emphasis added

ONE

Reawaken My Freedom

*Jesus, please reawaken my complete, absolute,
undivided, wholehearted freedom in You.*

Wherever the Spirit of the Lord is, there is freedom.

2 Corinthians 3:17

Dawn broke on a cool spring day. I was in a hurry to finish work-related items before leaving town with Troy for some much-needed rest together. Hustling to complete all my morning chores, I asked Troy, who was pouring a cup of coffee, if he wanted me to make a quick fire in our woodstove.

"No thanks," he responded. "I won't have time to enjoy it, but you can make one if you wish."

This was the first warmish morning in Central Oregon in a long time. The early spring had brought much snow and cold rain. Because the sunny morning was so inviting and I would be leaving soon, I decided for the first time of the year not to make a fire.

Troy rushed down the stairs and off to finish his remaining meetings.

I dashed into the kitchen, cleaned up the hasty breakfast mess and loaded all our gear into the waiting truck. Then I sat down with my Bible in my lap next to a cold woodstove.

Acknowledging before the Lord that my morning was all out of order, I apologized that I did not sit down with Him first, before all the morning hubbub. I prayed, read His Word and worshiped. His pleasure and presence flooded this sweet time together.

I had opened my Bible to a passage where the apostles were doing many miraculous signs and wonders (see Acts 5:12–42). Locals were bringing their sick and demon possessed to them, and all were healed.

The high priest and leading officials heard how everyone was flocking to these men and their loving message of hope and the powerful anointing upon them. Sadly, the leaders' selfish response was not one of reception but jealousy. When given the choice between self-justified pride or eternal hope, they rejected the hope that could heal them and clung to their pride, thus making pride their true god.

Reacting to the combustion of their own jealous envy, they persecuted the apostles for doing nothing more than healing the sick and speaking of hope in Jesus Christ. The apostles were doing exactly what He had commanded them to do and what the Holy Spirit was guiding them to do. And when they encountered deep-rooted pride, they were falsely accused and thrown into jail.

I was left to wonder about the collision of human pride and heavenly hope. I pondered why it is so hard to release our white-knuckled grip on what we think we know and simply trust God for what we do not.

Suddenly, I heard loud scratching and bumping over my head. The commotion was clearly coming from inside our stovepipe right at the apex where it exits our home. Our front room ceiling is vaulted, so the stovepipe is about fifteen feet high.

Clearly, something was stuck inside it. I could hear what could only be a bird falling deeper and deeper into a prison it could not escape. It labored for a long time, unable to fly in the tight space, its claws useless against the smooth steel.

Finally exhausted by a struggle it could not win, it fell the remaining distance into the large firebox. In an instinctual effort to escape this foreign place of pain, the bird slammed hard against the heavy glass door of our woodstove.

I knelt to look in at my unexpected captive, a female starling.

I recognized this species through cautionary tales from my grandfather. Despised, this invasive thief crowds out native birds by sheer number. They consume vast amounts of food sources and take over active nests built by smaller birds. Flying in great number, they devastate crops in minutes and leave behind droppings that can host disease. Their destructive behavior has earned them the negative collective reference of a "filth or scourge" of starlings. Preceded by such an unsavory reputation, perhaps some would let the bird before me die in her predicament.

I studied her through the sooty glass. She appeared exhausted from the fight and frightened to be in this ash-encrusted place.

There was no way out for her. She could not rescue, save or help herself. There was nothing she could do to improve her circumstances. She was a prisoner. Left in this dark, charred tomb, she would die.

My prayer was simple: *Holy Spirit, speak Your truth.*

I allowed the starling to rest for a moment while I contemplated how to release her. She needed to be calm, or she could perish in the struggle.

My solution was to drape an old towel over the front of the stove so the glass was covered and the box was completely dark. Donning a headlamp so there was only one direct source of light, I carefully opened the door. She was cowering in the very back of the box, hiding in the only way she could.

Slowly, I extended my hand toward her.

She did not move.

Tenderly, I placed my fingers around her tiny body and held her for a moment. She did not struggle and seemed to completely accept this new dilemma.

Gently, I withdrew my arm with a terrified bird in my palm. Blinking up into the light, she looked at me, and I looked at her.

She was beautiful. Perfect in every detail. Her feminine bill was long and slender. Her black eyes were shiny and alert. Although her deep-gray plumage was completely covered in ash, she appeared to be okay.

I walked out onto our deck and slowly opened my hand. I did not need to tell her what to do next. Hardwired with her life's purpose, she instantly flew away.

Here is what she did *not* do: fly back into captivity.

She did not rush over my shoulder into the house, back into the firebox and close the door. She recognized genuine freedom, chose it and never looked back.

If creation recognizes and chooses God's freedom, how much more should the sons and daughters of God?

In life, all of us face hard things. As we pursue God deeper into His will, at some point we will each end up in a charred prison of our own mistakes or another's prideful envy, false accusations and explosive rage. It is His light that exposes darkness and reveals sin.

When that happens, we have only two genuine ways in which we can respond. We can soften in the presence of His loving truth, repent of our sin and change direction. Or we can harden our hearts, reject His loving truth and continue headlong into the black prison of self-justification and pride.

When I peered into the firebox and saw the starling, I had a choice to make. I could love her by rescuing her . . . or reject her and let her die in the black tomb she had fallen into.

Likewise, when God the Father looked into the firebox of this world and saw me, covered in soot, doomed to die in the black prison of my sin, He chose love. And by His love, this life was rescued and released into His freedom. The Father's love always results in freedom—freedom from every prison.

Second Corinthians 3:16–17 proclaims this truth: "Whenever someone turns to the Lord, the veil is taken away. For the Lord is the Spirit, and wherever the Spirit of the Lord is, there is freedom."

Friend, the point of the encounter is this—you are that bird. Each of us is doomed to die, trapped within the filthy prison of our sin. But because of love, Jesus has entered your firebox and drawn you out. Now, it is the Prince of Peace who is holding you up before the light of the Father and opening His hand.

You have a choice to make.

You can squander your freedom and fly backward into the firebox of your human understanding. In this blackness, you are free to worship the idols of your pride, pain, guilt, shame, bitterness, complacency, anxiety, depression and unforgiveness. You can also blame others, even God, for the misery you suffer.

Or . . .

You can fly forward hard and fast into the loving purpose for which He created you.

"This means that anyone who belongs to Christ has become a new person. The old life is gone; a new life has begun! And all of this is a gift from God, who brought us back to himself through Christ" (2 Corinthians 5:17–18).

Indeed, the starling did not fly back into the firebox . . . and neither should we.

True redemption is hallmarked by a true *permanent* change of direction. Our transformed life should be proof of our transformed heart.

"Prove by the way you live that you have repented of your sins and turned to God," Jesus said (Matthew 3:8).

Friend, it is for freedom that Christ has set us free. Jesus did not endure the cross so that we would fly backward into the captivity of our past, our present or our selfish need to be "pursued" by God. Jesus has already done everything for us. All that is left for us to do, our singular responsibility, is to simply turn to Him and reach with all we have.

So we have not stopped praying for you since we first heard about you. We ask God to give you complete knowledge of his will and to give you spiritual wisdom and understanding. Then the way you live will always honor and please the Lord, and your lives will produce every kind of good fruit. All the while, you will grow as you learn to know God better and better. We also pray that you will be strengthened with all his glorious power so you will have all the endurance and patience you need. May you be filled with joy, always thanking the Father. He has enabled you to share in the inheritance that belongs to his people, who live in the light. For he has rescued us from the kingdom of darkness and transferred us into the Kingdom of his dear Son, who *purchased our freedom* and forgave our sins.

Colossians 1:9–14, emphasis added

In Him, we have complete freedom.

God's Word is true. Because of all Jesus has already done for us, we do not live in darkness—unless we choose to. The stone from Jesus' tomb, and ours, has been rolled away, shattered, crushed, destroyed. From that day forward, every dark place of suffering we will ever know in this life only has three sides. Nothing in this world can contain the freedom we have—except our own selfish desire to return and live in a three-sided tomb.

Often, the enemy uses our pain like a boomerang. We come before God and throw it away and experience His freedom. Then the enemy waits. He calculates the precise time to throw a "remembrance of prior pain" back toward us, like an ominous boomerang from our past.

We can keep standing in the truth that we are free and duck, letting his attack fly by without harm. Or we can choose to allow our prior anguish to clock us in the forehead. Once struck, most fall backward into the same position of angst that Jesus *just* freed them from. And this is where many believers choose to live: focused only on what was.

"What sorrow for those who drag their sins behind them with ropes made of lies, who drag wickedness behind them like a cart!" (Isaiah 5:18).

Friend, there is a reason God created us with eyes on the front of our heads and not the back. We were never made to look backward; we are designed to look forward. You cannot trip over what is behind you—unless you run back to it.

Paul wrote, "I focus on this one thing: *Forgetting the past and looking forward to what lies ahead*, I press on to reach the end of the race and receive the heavenly prize for which God, through Christ Jesus, is calling us" (Philippians 3:13–14, emphasis added).

Your doubt *is the thief* of His freedom.

The moment we doubt our release, we throw the boomerang with our own hand, and this becomes our circle back into captivity. "It is for freedom that Christ has set us free" (Galatians 5:1 NIV).

It is time to break your boomerang!

Today, many lean toward being defined by their torrent of pain—instead of His tsunami of peace.

"*Look straight ahead, and fix your eyes on what lies before you*. Mark out a straight path for your feet; stay on the safe path" (Proverbs 4:25–26, emphasis added).

As you walk into the freedom of Jesus, the hooks of pain the enemy throws at your back only have power when *you* empower them with your attention. When pain becomes your focus, it becomes your god, and you lose sight of the only One who can heal you.

The apostle Paul encourages, "We all, who with unveiled faces contemplate the Lord's glory, are being transformed into his image with ever-increasing glory, which comes from the Lord, who is the Spirit" (2 Corinthians 3:18 NIV). Simply stated, we become what we behold. If you want a painful life, keep focusing on your pain. If you want a free life in Jesus, keep focusing on *Him.* "The path of life leads upward for the wise; *they leave the grave behind*" (Proverbs 15:24, emphasis added). Beloved, it is time to leave the grave behind. You are free. You are free. You are free!

Because of love, Jesus came to this world. He reached into the blackness of your circumstances and drew you out into His light, love and life. Right now, His palm is open. Complete freedom awaits. May this be the day that His freedom within you is revived and reawakened. May this be the day that you choose to fly hard and fast into what has always been yours.

Jesus said, "You will know the truth, and the truth will set you free" (John 8:32). He alone is the way, truth and life; the more you purpose to know Him, the more freedom you will experience in every direction.

Friend, if Jesus is your Lord, you are already free.

Now is the time to ask Jesus to reveal the shackles of whatever has captured your attention and realign your life's focus on Him alone. Now is the time to stand up in His reawakened freedom within you . . . and start living as if you believe it is true.

Precious Jesus, today I reach for Your rescue.

I am dying in my sin, and in this place I cannot rescue, save or help myself.

Will You forgive me of my sin? Will You forgive me for choosing to focus more on my pain than on Your purpose?

I lift my broken heart to You and ask for Your truth to pour over it and wash away all the lies of the enemy.

Jesus, I acknowledge that genuine healing only comes from You—and I choose Your freedom.

Right now, I ask that You reveal my every hook of doubt, my every trigger of anger and my every boomerang of past pain.

I choose to bring them all before You. I acknowledge that the angst they produce is not my god—You are.

Today, I proclaim: Jesus Christ, You are my Lord and Savior. I lay my sin at Your feet and before my eyes. You are obliterating all of it with a single glance.

And now You are looking at me.

I feel the heat of Your love melting away every lie I believed over Your promises.

I sense my confinements falling off. The boomerangs and hooks are broken.

Your love always brings freedom for those who choose it.

Today, I choose to leave the grave behind and fly hard and fast into Your presence.

I am free. I am free. I am free!

You have rescued me because of Your love.

And because of Your love, I will live in Your freedom.

Thank You, thank You, thank You, precious Jesus.

Amen.

TWO

Reawaken My Pursuit of You

> *Jesus, please reawaken my passionate pursuit*
> *of our Father's rescue and refuge.*

Those who know your name trust in you, for you, Lord,
have never forsaken those who seek You.

Psalm 9:10 NIV

The wilderness is my passion. In this place, all the beeping,
buzzing and pinging stops, and there is only the song of
the wild. This is where I hear the voice of my God most clearly.
It is my truest church.

When you find your quiet, your personal place of stillness,
here you will find and know your God (see Psalm 46:10).

As often as I am able, I pursue Him in the remote places.
Within this vast expanse, I hunt. Sometimes I search for wild-
life, heart-filling vistas, beautiful stones, streams, waterfalls,
wind in the conifers, and sometimes I hunt for antlers that have
been shed. For this wild heart, I have learned that whatever I
am pondering, praying over, mulling through, to find an antler

among millions of acres of untamed land is a covenant from my heavenly Dad, declaring, *I've got that. I'm already answering your prayer. You can trust Me for it all.*

My beloved friend Sue is also passionate about scouring the high country for antlers. Years ago we made it an annual adventure. During our sojourns, we debrief all we are learning, our wrecks, our breakthroughs and our slow and sometimes painful growth into a deeper understanding of how to apply and live out God's Word. This beautiful process is the bedrock of each trip. And to find an antler during this time only strengthens the powerful lessons He is teaching us during these unique "heavenly Dad and daughter" interactions.

On our most recent shed-antler hunting trip, while lost in detailed conversation, her old truck seemed to intuitively know the way. Once again, we traveled to one of our favorite regions to explore. Affectionately called the "hallowed hills," this severely beautiful vertical terrain offers an isolated home for a strong number of Rocky Mountain elk. The familiarity of turning onto an old seemingly forgotten dirt road nearly felt like the long-awaited embrace of a treasured friend. Our ridiculous habit of excitement always draws us forward in our seats, perhaps to better see what we might discover around the next bend. I could not help but laugh at the sight of two grown women with noses nearly pressed against the windshield like housebound pups on their first mountain adventure.

Slowly, we pulled up to an unusual sight. To my dismay, I discovered that the only road leading into the hallowed hills wilderness was washed out and impassable. Backtracking, we threaded one abandoned logging road after another and finally found a suitable place to set up our base camp.

In no time, my dear friend had gathered pitch-laden deadwood and coaxed into existence her personal trademark: a roaring campfire. The next morning, we awoke to fresh-falling snow. The beauty and wonder called my heart by name. We could not get our packs on fast enough and go explore the frozen white message board at our feet. To hike where wild inhabitants tread, step for step, is such an extraordinary privilege.

In the days that followed, we explored country we had only previously seen from great distances. We climbed up and down terrain so steep that at times crawling would have been the safest option. We shimmied over slippery logs to cross streams so swollen by snowmelt that their normal happy chatter was transformed into roaring white torrents. We joined every breath of wind, every shaft of light, every glittering star in perpetual worship of the Creator of all.

Wanting to save the best adventure for our grand finale, we chose to make the challenging cross-country trek toward the hallowed hills. After a few hours of difficult hiking, we finally reached what has historically been our base camp. My heart swelled as I walked into what I can only describe as the living home of a beloved friend—safe, familiar, pouring out welcome and love.

Sue chose a line that was deeper down in the green folds of the ravine. I chose to stay higher and follow a fresh line of tracks. Soon a common sight captured my full attention below—a bone. Our God's precise balance of life ordains that wherever there are animals of prey, there will also be predators. I called down to Sue and communicated that I was going to descend toward her and investigate. Although I have examined countless kill sites, this one was different. Something was wrong. Instantly, the hair on my neck raised in primal alarm.

Trained by my grandfather, I read the environment around me. The scene was fresh, yielding a young cow elk taken down only a few days earlier. Her skeletal structure was nearly intact, still held together by strong ligaments. The ground was tossed and torn, giving silent witness of the mortal struggle. Then I noticed something that did not fit—a portion of a hind leg . . .

and then another, still covered with flesh and hair. There were too many legs.

Glancing around, I saw a second kill only yards from the first one. Evidenced by the long spiked antlers extending from his skull, this kill was a young bull. A large gut pile lay only a few steps down the slope. A kill on top of a kill. Food was still on the ground. My mind raced. Only one predator hunts and kills like this, but the official status in Oregon tracks only a few. Suddenly, my eyes riveted on a single unmistakable warning. In my earlier haste to read the scene, I had missed it. Strategically placed on the skull of the cow was feces—canine feces.

This was a wolf attack.

Only a coordinated hunt by a pack could bring down multiple prey of this size. The signature threat of defecating on a skull is feral canine for, *This kill is mine. If you touch it, I will kill you too!*

Meat was still on the ground around me. Wolves would not leave that behind. I had walked into their kill zone and potentially scattered them. My ever-heightening sense was that they were close, very close, perhaps just beyond my sight . . . watching.

Quickly, I called Havee, my small female Blue Heeler pup, to my feet. Responding in mirrored unison, Sue called Chaco, her male working dog, to come in close. Together, we stood up straight and walked through the carnage.

In the next quarter of a mile, we found six more kills. Clearly, wolves had moved into the hallowed hills.

As scheduled, the following day we packed up our gear and began the long journey out of the wilderness. When our tires finally hit pavement, we were still discussing all the events of our previous trek. By following the course of the river, the motion of the truck felt like a smooth, comforting pendulum as we swung around one opposing turn after another.

While rounding a great bend, an unexpected sight interrupted our conversation. Instinctively, Sue pressed the brakes. Appearing lost in this wild land were two cattle dogs pacing in the road before us. Rolling to a stop near them, we could see they were panting heavily and near complete exhaustion. I opened the truck door and quietly stepped out.

A quick evaluation of the scene revealed what appeared to be two primarily black-and-white border collie–type dogs. One was an older male, and the second was a much younger female. The male was shaking hard in the hind end and near collapse. The female was stronger but timid. I knelt and encouraged the lost dogs to come to me.

Without hesitation, the old male came right over. He was far beyond his physical abilities and recognized the help. After reassuring him for a moment, I took a few steps back to the truck and patted the floorboards, inviting him to jump in.

He tried but was too exhausted. Instead, still panting hard, he looked right at my face as if to ask, *Will you help me? I'm too weak. Will you lift me into your rescue?*

Carefully, I scooped up his trembling hind end and boosted him up onto the seat.

Realizing she was now alone, the younger female anxiously circled the truck. Again, I knelt and encouraged her to come to me. Step for cautious step, she came.

I gently placed my hand on the back of her neck and made the same motions a mother dog would to comfort her pup.

She was still panting hard but trusted me enough to sit down. Our confidence-building communication continued until she started to blink freely, and her frightened eyes softened with the desire to trust.

The moment her focus shifted from fear to trust, I tenderly picked her up and placed her into the safety of the truck.

The journey toward home continued with the addition of two lost souls who had just been found.

Within this wild land, my first thought was that someone had abandoned the dogs. But over the miles, while firmly planted in a complete stranger's lap, they proved to be kind, well trained and mannerly. These dogs were loved. Someone was missing part of their family.

Together, Sue and I prayed, asking Jesus what to do next. In scattered silence, we drove more than fifty miles to the nearest town. The tiny rural establishment had about the same number of people. In this tight-knit community, someone had to know about these pups.

Sue headed to the post office, and I dashed to the only restaurant in town. Then, she went to the gas station, and I went to the tiny store. Having just covered the entire town, we pursued two men who were working outdoors. One turned out to be the mayor, and the other was the county sheriff. They were as delightful as one would expect small-town officials to be. Thrilled to share their funny stories with fresh ears, they amused us with their informal banter.

Together we came up with a plan to take the dogs on to the next town, another thirty or so miles away. They assured us of a veterinarian there who had the capability to foster the dogs and send out county-wide bulletins. While shaking the mayor's hand, I told him I was so thankful that we found them because I did not believe they would have survived the night. He looked at me with obvious curiosity.

I explained the tenuous scene we had encountered only the day before.

Without words, he and the sheriff exchanged glances.

I continued, "I know that officially, there are only a few reported wolves in Oregon . . . but I know what I saw."

He glanced up toward the direction from which we had come. "Well, you never know."

I smiled and respectfully added, "Well, actually . . . I do know." I then explained how my grandfather had taught me about the wilderness, tracks, reading the environment and especially how to identify predators. "*That* is wolf scat." I showed him a photo of the feces-covered skull I had taken.

He passed my phone to the sheriff, who raised his eyebrows and nodded at the same time.

The mayor pointed up the valley. "It's hard to deny their presence when we see 'em runnin' through the neighbor's pastures right over there. And a rancher upriver where you were yesterday sees the pack you encountered often. They're here all right. And who can blame them. The elk population in our county has exploded. We're glad they're back to reestablish the natural balance."

After Sue and I thanked them for their wise counsel, we headed to the gas station to top off the tank with fuel. I jogged to the store to tell the residents of our plans with the dogs, then headed back to the truck.

I looked up to see a tearful reunion in progress.

"It's the owner of the dogs!" Sue exclaimed. "He was only in town for minutes to drop off some work with the mayor, who then pointed toward our truck and told him two dogs were found in the region of his off-grid homestead." She beamed. "Can you believe it?"

In the frenzy of elated conversation that followed, we learned how the owner of the dogs commanded them to stay home on the porch while he dashed into town. The dogs disobeyed him and traveled cross-country approximately twelve miles from the safety of their home.

What should have ended in tragedy *did not*.

Do you see the parable?

Had the dogs not gotten into the truck, complete annihilation would have been their fate. The dogs had to *trust* us to get into the truck to be returned to the one who loved them most. Had they rejected our offer, they would have been destroyed by the wolves.

◆ ◆ ◆

In Matthew 7, Jesus warns us to watch out for those who proclaim a message that sounds close to the truth but is not the truth. They speak a false hope that leads away from the Father's love. They look like "harmless sheep but are really vicious wolves" (v. 15). Later in Matthew, Jesus calls us "sheep among wolves" (10:16).

This strong movement toward fake hope demands that God should pursue us (He already has—He sent His Son). The true danger of this belief is if God needs to pursue us, it only means one thing—our back is turned to Him because we are running away from His presence toward something we value more. Fake freedom teaches that believers can live on the redline of this world, with one foot on "belief in Jesus" and the other entrenched in what offends holiness. Yet in this position, the enemy has access to attack anytime he chooses.

This is not faith; it is spiritual roulette.

When we leave the safety of our Father's presence, every step we take away from Him only leads us deeper into wolf territory. Are you pursuing Jesus' genuine freedom? Or are you meandering toward "fake freedom" that leads away from His presence into a deadly ambush?

Perhaps you are like the lost pups and your haphazard steps have led you into a wilderness of fear and uncertainty. In every direction, you encounter snarling teeth. Maybe you are being attacked, bitten, torn apart by the very ones you love. It is possible that you are the one lost in a wasteland of confusion, bitterness, pride, selfishness, depression, anxiety, anger, unforgiveness, and without rescue you know you will not survive.

Wolves are coming and, in fact, are already here.

Beloved, this is what is true: The rescue truck of God's love for you is here now. The door is open, and Jesus Himself waits with arms open wide, patting the floorboards of His Father's love, inviting you to jump in.

Will you? Will you choose to remain lost in a wolf-infested wilderness? Or will you choose to be found in the Father's love?

Genuine rescue begins with genuine pursuit of God's open door. No matter what you face, if you want help, it is time to get in the truck!

"If you look for me *wholeheartedly*, you will find me" (Jeremiah 29:13, emphasis added).

God is not interested in *part* of your heart. He desires for you to pursue Him with *all* your heart. Giving Him only part of your heart is the same as giving Him part of your cancer. The rest of it is still going to kill you. He does not want to heal part of you; He wants to heal *all* of you. Likewise, giving Him only part of your heart would be the same as trying to lead *part* of a horse. Until the *whole* horse decides to follow, you are not going anywhere.

In the same way, our heavenly Father does not want to redeem, heal and free only part of your heart, a portion of your soul, a bit of your mind and a piece of your strength. Complete renewal before God begins when you stop pursuing God with your parts and pieces and start pursuing Him with your all. If you genuinely want to move deeper into the loving presence of God, pursue Him with all of your heart.

"So I say to you: Ask and it will be given to you; seek and you will find; knock and the door will be opened to you. For everyone who asks receives; the one who seeks finds; and to the one who knocks, the door will be opened" (Luke 11:9–10 NIV). Ask, seek, knock, press in, chase. These are pursuant words of action—actions we can all do.

The point of the encounter is this: The dogs wandered away from the safety of their master and knew they were in trouble. When help was offered, they accepted it and were reunited with the one who loved them most. It would have been foolishness to chase the second dog around the truck to *make* her get in; she had to trust first and then choose to get in.

It is not Jesus' job to chase us, because our back is to Him as we run away. In Matthew 14:30, when Peter was sinking into oblivion, he cried out to Jesus for help. Jesus' hand was instantly within reach. Peter took it and was instantly saved.

You and I can be, too.

Someone who truly wants genuine rescue will leap into it when it is offered. So the real question is this: Do you want genuine rescue that leads to genuine refuge in His presence?

Again, in 2 Chronicles 7:14 we read, "Then if my people who are called by my name will *humble themselves and pray and seek my face and turn from their wicked ways*, I will hear from heaven and will forgive their sins and restore their land" (emphasis added).

Every minute of every day, we can choose to humble ourselves, and pray, and seek His face and turn from our pain. When we choose to turn toward Him and pursue Him over our troubles, that is when He hears our cry, forgives our wayward choices and heals our hearts.

Just like the lost dogs, you and I have a responsibility—we must choose to *get in the truck.*

But first we must admit that we need help and release our control (humble ourselves). We must ask our heavenly Dad for help (pray). We must pursue Him (seek His face), and we must abandon our wayward journey in the wrong direction (turn). When we choose to humble ourselves, pray, seek Him and turn from our junk, *then* God hears, forgives, heals.

The pursuit of Him comes first. The rescue, forgiveness and healing refuge come second.

Without humbly recognizing their need, asking for help through their actions, seeking to get into the truck and turning away from their errant direction, the dogs would have been annihilated by the wolves. Without the same response, you and I face the same annihilation.

Friend, the shelter of the master's love was always there for the pups. They left it, and genuine rescue brought them back. Genuine rescue for us happens when we literally pursue and jump into the Father's love. And genuine refuge follows—when we stay there.

Know that the shelter of the Father's love for you is here now. You have an "ever-present help" in time of need (Psalm 46:1 NIV). Always.

It is our responsibility to seek the Father's loving presence and then stay in His presence. If you are not experiencing His help, it is for one reason only—*you* are not choosing it.

All the enemy truly cares about is you jumping out of God's protective presence. Once you are away from the loving shelter of the Almighty, the enemy's singular focus is your continual slide toward utter destruction. He wants everything in you that belongs to Jesus to die. Whether slow or quick makes no difference to him; our enemy is always watching and waiting for an avenue to attack and destroy. His endgame is to run you down into a spiritual massacre so complete that the horrifying result will be his defecation on your skull.

"Temptation comes from our own desires, which *entice us and drag us away*. These desires give birth to sinful actions. And when sin is allowed to grow, it gives birth to death" (James 1:14–15, emphasis added).

Friend, the spiritual direction of your life is no game.

Light and darkness cannot share the same place within any heart; we are either running to Jesus or away (see Matthew 12:30; 2 Corinthians 6:14).

"In Christ we have *bold and confident access to God* through faith in him" (Ephesians 3:12 CEB, emphasis added).

In Christ, in His presence, is where closeness to God begins.

This world's fake faith is the result of turning away from the One who rescues and turning toward our own selfishness, thereby rejecting the direction our Dad is driving. Fake faith is fed every time we are enticed by the enemy's temptations zooming by the window. It grows when our focus shifts away from the protection of God's loving presence, and we jump out the window to pursue things that lead us away from Him.

Fake faith says, *This is okay.*

Real faith says, *This will get you killed.*

Beloved, it is time to say no to fake faith and yes to the genuine pursuit of His presence. Why? Because we cannot know genuine revival with a divided heart.

No one can ride in the truck with the Father and jump out the window at the same time. We each pursue what is most important to us. If our back is turned to the One we call God because we still want to run with wolves, we will never know the fullness of His rescue or refuge in His loving presence.

When it comes to pursuing His genuine rescue and genuine refuge, we need to get in the truck and *stay* in the truck (see John 15:4). So why pursue? Because rarely do we find what we are *not* looking for. Genuine rescue happens once we look for it.

And genuine revival is motivated by genuine love for God over all other things. Love for His presence drives us to pursue Him above all else. And wholehearted pursuit is what leads to the rescue and refuge of your heart.

Today, will you get in the truck?

Precious Jesus, I don't want to jump out of Your presence anymore.

I'm done running after fake religion that only serves my selfish need to be pursued.

I acknowledge that every step I take away from You leads me deeper into the ambush of the enemy.

In this wilderness, my heart is fearful of the wolves, and my body is exhausted from the pain.

I have wandered from the loving protection of my Master, and my prodigal heart is coming home.

Today, I leave behind my meandering half-heartedness that was once my relationship with You.

Right now, I give You all that I am—heart, soul, mind, strength.

Jesus, I choose to follow only You. I'm running and jumping into Your arms.

Will You lift me into the rescue and refuge of Your beautiful presence?

Today, I commit to pursue You alone.

I humbly receive Your rescue.

Gratefully, I will remain in Your refuge.

My heart is safe within Your heart.

For the rest of my days, nearness to You is what I desire.

Thank You, my Savior.

THREE

Reawaken My Love

Jesus, Your love breaks through every boundary of darkness in the hearts of men. Please reawaken my love. Help me to see the unseen through Your eyes of love.

Dear friends, let us continue to love one another, for love comes from God. Anyone who loves is a child of God and knows God. But anyone who does not love does not know God, for God is love. God showed how much he loved us by sending his one and only Son into the world so that we might have eternal life through him. This is real love—not that we loved God, but that he loved us and sent his Son as a sacrifice to take away our sins. Dear friends, since God loved us that much, we surely ought to love each other.

1 John 4:7–11

It was early in the day and I was rushing to finish up some errands in a small town near our ranch. Assuming I was finished, I started to leave and was suddenly "reminded" that I needed to swing into a gas station and fuel up my truck. On this cold morning, I was grateful that Oregon remains one of the few states where it is illegal to pump your own gas.

As I turned into the familiar station, an unfamiliar man approached to pump my fuel. The Holy Spirit highlighted him. Curious as to what the Lord wanted me to see, I watched him intently.

He was thin and disheveled. His clothing was filthy and too big. His demeanor portrayed a difficult life. But what struck me most was his obvious aversion to look at me eye to eye. He appeared to be hiding, unseen in plain sight. He acted as if he were invisible and wanted to stay that way.

Instantly, visions of Jesus walking the lonely shores and plying the back alleys flashed through my mind. He was looking for the forgotten so He could lavish them with His love. I sensed the sweetest laughter and heard a nearly audible, *Go get him!*

My silent prayer was nothing more than, *Holy Spirit, lead me. What does this son need?*

Through mind-numbing monotony, and still not looking at my eyes, the attendant asked what I needed, took my keys and card, and began the process of fueling my truck. It was cold, and as soon as he returned my things, he stood nearby with his hands pushed down as deep into his tattered pockets as they would allow.

I sensed the Spirit say, *He needs to laugh.*

Hmm, Lord, this could be tricky. He doesn't look like he wants to laugh.

Not knowing where to begin, I engaged him with simple affirmation. "Thank you, sir, for the service. On this cold day, I so appreciate it."

Without looking my way, he nodded and made a *huh* sound.

Not giving up, I pressed in. "No really, I get to sit in my warm truck and you are so kind to serve me and everyone else who drives up. And you do it with really cold hands.

How do you even do that? You must have some sort of hidden superpower!"

Then, like an errant flash of lightning, the corner of his mouth rose . . . and fell. "I don't know of anything I do that's special," he said, still avoiding my gaze.

Carefully, I stepped through his open door. "Brother, are you kidding me? I couldn't do your job for a day! I'd have this place so messed up! Do you know how many trucks I'd blow up by putting in the wrong fuel?"

The thought of that ridiculous image made him crack a smile. Instantly, he covered his mouth with his hand. But first, I saw what he was trying to hide—he had no teeth.

I wanted to jump out of my truck and hug him. Instead, not wanting to overwhelm him, I compared his abilities to a super-hero on a secret mission to save Central Oregon trucks from certain disaster by falling into the hands of someone like me.

Enjoying the humor, he started telling me funny stories of what people do and say at his station.

By the time the fuel pump clicked off, we were both laughing like old buddies.

"Do you want your receipt, ma'am?" he asked through sub-siding laughter.

"No, I don't need it. But I do need to tell you something. My precious little grandma used to always say, 'Kind thoughts are wasted if they don't become kind words.' So I need to honor my grandmother and tell you my kind thought. You have a great smile! Brother, don't ever stop smiling."

Then he looked right at me. The weathered lines of his smudged face softened, and without a word, he nodded. The arrow of Jesus' love had been released. And it always hits its target.

In the season following that first encounter, I would go to this same gas station as often as I could. Equally often, my slender friend would stop what he was doing and greet me in grand fashion.

Over time our conversations deepened from silly to real. He experienced Jesus' love through this vessel. And that was enough for him to lean toward that flame of compassion and return the greatest gift he had—he would burst out the most glorious toothless, waving, warm-eyed smile heaven has ever seen—because *he* was seen. A gas station attendant in a tiny mountain town was completely transformed.

The almighty love of Jesus can do this for anyone who chooses to receive it. His uncontainable, unstoppable, unfathomable love is the greatest weapon of warfare we carry, and it fills every vacuum into which we release it. Our singular challenge is to see the need, step forward in faith and release His love in whatever unique and beautiful way He desires.

The need for the outpouring of Jesus' healing love is all around us. As many times as I have recognized it and stepped forward into releasing His greatest gift, there have been a zillion more times when I was so wrapped up in my world, my schedule, my busyness that I moved right on by without a backward glance. No compassion was delivered. No light was released. No heart was impacted by the only love that can truly heal.

The love of God is *so* vital in this world that Jesus Himself said, "I am giving you a new commandment: Love each other. Just as I have loved you, you should love each other. Your love for one another will prove to the world that you are my disciples" (John 13:34–35). Again, He tells His disciples, "This is my commandment: Love each other in the same way I have loved you" (15:12).

The application is, friend: What are your actions proving? Are you running past or running toward those in need? Are you recognizing that Jesus' love, through you, is the greatest gift you can give your world?

Throughout the gospels and beyond, Jesus proved through His life that every miracle was motivated by the same almighty force—love.

Whether you see it or not, the outpouring of God's love transforms every environment it is released into, beginning with the vessel that carries it. I have experienced His love pour out in astonishing ways and seen the dead rise, limbs grow, spines heal, bone deformities straighten and lethal illnesses instantly reverse. And I have experienced His love pour out in even simpler ways: through a smile, a kind word, a hug, a text, a call, a handful of flowers or a plate of homemade cookies.

Indeed, when our God's love is released, whether astonishing or simple, the miracle of His presence follows.

Releasing His love is not hard. Jesus has already done the work.

We are simply called to follow His example (see Ephesians 5:1). He went to where the hurting people were, and amid their brokenness, He loved them mightily. His purposeful intention to release the Father's love is what transformed the world around Him.

This is what He is calling you to do.

"For the LORD your God is living among you. He is a mighty savior. He will take delight in you with gladness. With his love, he will calm all your fears. He will rejoice over you with joyful songs" (Zephaniah 3:17).

God's love is with us. It is mighty. He delights in us. He calms our fears. He sings over us with joy.

The love of God will fill any painful black vacuum we release it into. This is our job and our joy. And because of what Jesus did, we get to treasure the outcome.

The love of God is the most powerful force in all human history, the most powerful force period. Jesus did not endure the cross so we could sip from this omnipotent "well of life" like scalding tea; He crashed through death and sin so we could drink from the fire hose of God's presence.

Friend, who among the unseen, or those who carry unseen pain, would not wish for this kind of love?

Jesus said, "Those who accept my commandments and obey them are the ones who love me. And because they love me, my Father will love them. And I will love them and reveal myself to each of them" (John 14:21). It is not enough to know what we should do when it comes to Jesus' love. If we truly love Him, we will truly love others like He did. And when we do, He will reveal Himself to us.

Revelation comes through obedience. The more we obey Him, the more we experience His presence. *That* is the foundation of love itself.

An unseen gas station attendant in a tiny mountain town, unseen grocery clerks, unseen neighbors, unseen students, unseen families—the unseen are all around us every day.

Will you see them? Will you allow the Father to break through your blindness and see the unseen with His love?

Jesus, Your love breaks through every boundary of darkness in the hearts of men. Please reawaken my love. Help me to see the unseen through Your eyes of love.

Precious Savior,
It is Your love that has broken through my darkness.
It is Your love that has redeemed me.
It is Your love that I now carry.
There is no defense against this almighty power.
It is the greatest weapon of warfare I possess.
Jesus, open my eyes to the force that is Your love.
I stand on the truth that to obey You leads to revelation of Your loving presence.

May I become more sensitive to Your Spirit than to my schedule.

Break through my blindness and open my eyes to see the unseen—all of them.

I offer all that I am to all that You are.

Pour Your love through me.

Transform the hurting around me by its glorious flood.

Jesus, today I beg You to reawaken Your love in me.

Amen.

SECTION TWO

RESTORE MY SOUL

Jesus replied, "The most important commandment is this: 'Listen, O Israel! The LORD our God is the one and only LORD. And you must love the LORD your God with all your heart, all your *soul* . . .'"

Mark 12:29–30, emphasis added

FOUR

Restore My Trust

*Jesus, because You will never, ever let go, in
You alone may my trust be wholly restored.*

Those who know your name trust in you, for you, O
LORD, do not abandon those who search for you.

Psalm 9:10

I belong to a beloved group made up of three dear sisters in
Christ and me: Kelly, Kai, Kacy and Kim. Affectionately
known as the "Quad-K," each time one of us reaches a decadal
birthday, we all gather to celebrate by surprising the birthday
girl with a fun trip suited toward one of her passions. Since
Kacy loves to hike, when her turn came, we surprised her with
a trip to Moab, Utah, a true "God of Wonders" place.

One of our areas of exploration was the Devil's Garden region in Arches National Park, a wonderful place to experience
hiking on slickrock. Resulting from a bygone sea, slickrock
is the petrified compilation of sand and sediments that looks
like massive dinosaur backs. They range from several inches to

several hundred feet in height. The resulting "fins" are so seamless and smooth that most can be easily scaled with nothing more than grippy-treaded running shoes.

Shouldering our packs, we set out for the six-and-a-half-mile trek into the majesty of this amazing world. The sand, glorious in color and texture, was so fine that the passage of every living thing was captured in extraordinary detail. We marveled at the perfection of lizard, mouse and insect tracks, adding our own footprints to this wondrous billboard of silent communication.

Soon our trail turned upward, and we began the awe-inspiring process of moving through enormous fins of golden slickrock. Navigating this unique stone is a fun challenge because it requires the hiker to stand up straight. *Focus on the top, trust your feet not to slip and move with intention.* Laughing to myself, I conceded this type of hiking is probably as close to a Spiderman performance as I will ever get.

We were halfway up a thirty-foot section of slickrock when I heard an uneasy cry behind me. I turned to see one of my gregarious sisters crumpled into a crouching position. She was moving her palms over the rock, searching for an imperfection to grip. Without looking up, she quietly repeated to herself, a tremor in her voice, "I can't do this. I just can't *do* this."

Something was wrong.

I carefully turned around and negotiated the few steps between us. The other two were climbing closer to Kacy and were already crouching on either side of her in support.

Easing my way back to her, I ventured, "Are you all right? What's wrong?"

"I'm afraid," she said after a moment. "Afraid of heights!"

What? My mind jammed. How was it possible I had known this woman most of my life and did not know this about her? And now, as a gift I was leading her higher and higher up the slickrock fins.

My prayer was little more than, *Lord, show me which way to go.*

Together, perched sideways on a slope of slickrock, we concluded that she would be safe to sit on her heels and carefully scoot down. After mustering the remaining shreds of her courage, she did just that.

Once we were all safely reunited at the base of the rock, we chose alternate routes and made our way through some of the most spectacular country known to humankind. Late in the day, we reached the very top of the trail system. Through the waning light, we saw the parking lot far below.

But one fin of slickrock remained between us and our destination.

Kelly and Kai scaled the rock and searched along the top, looking for an easier ascent, while Kacy and I moved along the base searching for the same thing. The fin was somewhat uniform in height and quite long. Each end dropped off into treacherous canyons.

A simple prayer rotated within my heart. *Lead me, Holy Spirit.*

After scouting the entire length of the stony fin, Kacy and I were on our way back to rejoin Kelly and Kai on the crest when the Spirit prompted me to look up. From this return angle, I could see where someone had strategically placed a dead tree trunk in a dip of the fin in the most climbable angle.

I looked at the solution and smiled. Whether the tree was placed by another acrophobic hiker or Jesus Himself, either way He had provided the means for escape.

I climbed up first to assess the situation. The lower part of the tree was relatively straight and easy to shimmy up. But the upper portion was crooked, making it wobbly when supporting moving weight. Climbing a precarious log would not be too difficult by itself. But since the tippy section was suspended about ten feet off the ground, this was going to be a challenge for my height-sensitive loved one.

Wobbly and tippy places in the wilderness are just part of the adventure. But for someone who has not had that consistent opportunity, this would not be adventurous—it would be terrifying.

A heavy, unspoken truth hung between us. The sun was going down, and she could not remain where she was. There was no way to go around what she feared. She knew what she needed to do and was steeling herself to find the courage, the *trust*, to press through her barrier of fear.

Squaring up on my hands and knees, I positioned myself on the stone at the top of the tree trunk. Armed with the minimal information I had gained while scaling the snag, I told her what she could expect. The climb would be easy at first, then a little tippy on the top but solid.

Kacy nodded, then started the climb with focused determination. As expected, she ascended the lower part of the leaning tree with confidence. With each push up the log, she inched closer and closer to the nearly flat stony spot upon which I waited. Looking up, she grasped the first crooked bend and tried to balance herself in this unknown position.

The entire log rocked under her weight.

Her instant rebalance was to look down and collapse onto the log chest first. Her limbs drew tightly toward her center; fear was galvanizing her body into something as rigid as the snag she clung to.

We were only a few feet apart.

"I can't, I can't, I can't do this!" she murmured.

Holy Spirit, help us! I prayed. *We need You now!*

True to His nature, He was already present and waiting for the invitation to lead. His peace enveloped us.

With my heart steadied by *His* presence, I spoke to my beloved friend. "Look at me. You're going to be all right. I'm going to reach down, and we're going to lock wrists. At the count of three, I'm going to pull you up onto this rock."

Looking intently at my face, Kacy agreed wordlessly. She reached up, and I reached down and gripped her wrist.

"Are you ready?" I asked.

She nodded yes. As tightly as I held her wrist, her grip was even stronger.

I started the count. "One . . . two . . ."

Suddenly, her voice cut through. "Wait! Wait! Wait!" She looked right at me. Her eyes flooded with liquid fear. "Promise that you've got me! Promise that you won't let me fall! Promise that you won't let go!"

Tears of affirmation filled my eyes. "I promise." I repeated, "Are you ready?"

Again, she nodded.

"One . . . two . . . three!" I pulled hard, leaning backward with my combined weight and strength.

She let go of the tree trunk and literally leaped toward the fin. In a single smooth motion, my precious sister landed facedown on the solid rock next to me. Pure relief poured out from both of us as we wept side by side. Immediately, the other girls gathered around her in the sweetest familial support.

Rising to my feet, I looked at the three, who were now bound together in a sincere triple hug. Without shifting the scene, the Holy Spirit suddenly allowed me to see something. It was an "overlay" of His truth. Like a beautiful drawing on crystal-clear glass, it fit perfectly over what just happened.

Suddenly, I was the one lying facedown on the stone. All humanity was facedown on the stone.

Beloved, do you understand this is what I wish to do with all who are Mine?

I am calling every son and daughter to break off the focus on their circumstances.

Look up at My face.
I am already reaching for them.
And I desire all to reach for Me.
Pure trust will consume the desire to cling to that which will destroy you.
I want to pull you through your tippy, fearful, prideful places up onto the Solid Rock of My presence.
Release your human understanding and control and let go!
Place your hand in Mine!
Leap into My presence!
Look at My face. Look at My face. Look at My face!
Here, there is no instability, only trust!

To this day, that moment with my courageous loved one remains one of the most powerful demonstrations of genuine trust I have ever witnessed. I would not have learned it had she backed down. She proved what trusting God looks like—letting go of the counterfeits and leaping toward Christ.

She reached up. He reached down. This is the powerful blueprint of the place where trust is forged—when we choose to release our white-knuckled grip on what we think we know, what we think will help us, and reach for the hand of the One who is help incarnate.

"This is my command—be strong and courageous! Do not be afraid or discouraged. For the Lord your God is with you wherever you go" (Joshua 1:9).

God is with us. We do not face a single minute of terror alone. Because He is with us, and He is not afraid to leap, neither should we.

Most of us think we trust God—right up until we do not. Trust is not a thought or feeling; it is an action. We cannot say we trust God and remain immobile, stuck in our junkyard of lies.

"Come close to God, and God will come close to you. . . . Humble yourselves before the Lord, and he will lift you up in honor" (James 4:8, 10).

The first step of the revival of our trust is to humble ourselves before God and admit that we trust "things" more than Him. This might sound harsh, but the truth is, trusting things is nearly the definition of idolatry.

That which we trust is that which we follow—and that which we serve. If what we trust is not God, this is where we start. The revival of *our* trust does not begin near us; it begins in us. True ignition happens when we choose, we purpose, we take action to move closer to the One who holds us securely.

Instead of causing us to sink into the enemy's pitfall of failure, these terrifying moments can become the most hallowed experiences of our lives. Every realization of what we fear is a holy opportunity to move forward through it. The closer we move to Him, the more secure our hearts become. Like a fledgling eagle, we get to choose to lean into the wind of the Holy Spirit, open our wings and leap into the everlasting glory of a deeper trust in the One who loves us most.

How do we know when we are truly in this place? Our hearts flood with peace. And no matter what evil, black, fanged grimace we face, there is only rest. Our level of peace is the true barometer of our trust.

My precious grandmother's favorite Bible passage is one most know well, yet often do not *do* well: "Trust in the LORD with all your heart; do not depend on your own understanding. Seek his will in all you do, and he will show you which path to take" (Proverbs 3:5–6).

Pretty clear. God wants you to trust Him with *all* your heart, not just the bits you can still do yourself if He does not show up within your time frame. From this stance rises the mindset, *Wow! God really showed up!* The truth is, He is omnipresent (everywhere all the time). The real phrase should be, *Wow! I finally showed up! I finally trusted His Spirit and experienced His presence in a deeper way.*

God the Father, Jesus the Son and the Holy Spirit are "the same yesterday, today, and forever" (Hebrews 13:8). We serve the same God. We are redeemed with the same blood of Jesus. We are filled with the same Holy Spirit. Once we trust this truth, once we trust Him, our tippy places of fear and doubt will transform into the bridge that leads into permanent, whole-hearted faith and courage within His presence.

If, however, we choose to view the world through our shaky circumstances, the result is a shaky life of anxiety. By choosing to view our King through our shaky circumstances, the result is His Spirit through us crushing all anxiety. What once produced fear will instead produce faith. What once inspired terror will instead inspire trust.

So how do you know when you are genuinely trusting Him—or still stuck in a tippy place of not trusting?

Easy. Wherever fear resides in your life, this is what you are not trusting God for.

God's Word is clear. "Perfect love casts out fear" (1 John 4:18 NKJV). And guess who perfect love is? The answer is found in verse 16: "God is love." Wherever fear is, God is not.

Light and darkness cannot share the same place (see 2 Corinthians 6:14). Wherever God is, fear is not.

Fear is like a railroad crossing, where flashing red lights warn that you are not trusting God completely. Once engaged, it roots deeply into works of the flesh and builds a foundation that is locked in human effort.

Fear is the honest reflection that you are still trying to manipulate an outcome through your own understanding. Fear, *anxiety*, is a demonic diversion that seethes, *You cannot trust God.*

Fear and faith cannot occupy the same place within any heart.

Friend, words mean nothing. The real answer of where trust lies is revealed through actions. Are you clinging to the tippy place you know? Or are you reaching through your challenging circumstances and slapping your wrist into Jesus', fully believing He will not only draw you through them, but even better, draw you deeper into *His* presence.

When you choose to release your fearful doubt and reach, actually leap, for the ever-present hand of your God, a supernatural transference takes place. You will know when this happens, because all fear will melt before the presence of your King into beautiful, powerful, abiding *trust.*

It is His desire that your trust become so foundational that when the tippy places arise and your heart pleads, *Promise that You've got me! Promise that You won't let me fall! Promise that You won't let go!* you can rest in knowing He has got you. He will not let you fall, and He will never, ever let go.

Beloved, the restoration of your trust begins when you choose to reach up, knowing He is always reaching down. By choosing Him, in a single smooth leap you can move from your tippy log onto His solid rock of love for you. And within this sacred place, with your wrist firmly slapped in His, no matter the circumstances, there is only peace.

This is how trust works.

"Those who know your name trust in you, for you, O LORD, do not abandon those who search for you" (Psalm 9:10).

Precious Savior,

On this day, I get to choose between remaining in my tippy places of anxiety or choosing the Rock that is You.

I acknowledge that You've got me, that You won't let me fall, that You won't let go.

Jesus, before You, I name my fears, my tippy places, and I choose to no longer live clinging to them. Today, I choose to cling to You.

In this moment, I purpose to stop focusing on my fear and to start focusing on Your beautiful face.

No longer will I glorify my fear more than I glorify You.
No longer will I serve my fear more than I serve You.
Right now, I choose to slap my hand in Yours, and leap
deeper into Your presence . . . onto the Rock that is You.
Get ready to catch me, Jesus.
Because today, I choose Your trust.
I choose You!
Amen.

FIVE

Restore My Faith

*Jesus, restore my faith. I don't want
to be faithless any longer.*

"Don't be faithless any longer. Believe!"

John 20:27

Cathy's journey to Crystal Peaks Youth Ranch began on a cold winter morning while listening to the radio program *Focus on the Family*. Across the airwaves, she learned the story of our beginnings.

Ten years after the death of my parents, I met and married the love of my life, Troy, then we moved to Central Oregon and bought the only property we could afford, an abandoned cinder mine. Soon after, we rescued two horses, who quickly became the catalyst for everything that Jesus had planned all along. In 1995, we founded Crystal Peaks Youth Ranch, a unique ministry that rescues abused and neglected horses and pairs them with hurting kids. Since that time, the ranch has rescued over three hundred horses and serves about five thousand visitors annually, most of whom are kids. All come free of charge. The ranch also supports the families of the children who participate through several means, including Refuge, an enormous family gathering, potluck, worship and simple Gospel teaching. Crystal Peaks has also helped to shoulder into existence about 220 similar ranch ministries throughout the United States, Canada and a dozen in foreign nations.

Intrigued, she wondered if her ranch could do something similar.

By visiting our website, she discovered that we have an annual four-day IGNITION conference in the spring. As a participant, she would gain assistance and spiritual support in sorting out the nuts and bolts of how to start her own ministry. She was excited to learn how to provide an opportunity for individuals to connect with horses as a means to experience the love of God and discover His Word.

Unfortunately, six weeks before her trip from Canada, she contracted a vicious flu that triggered vertigo so extreme that she needed a walker to stand. Her doctor warned that flying was out of the question, and she feared she would have to cancel. So she prayed, and as only He can, the Lord parted the sea of impossibility and made a way for her to come.

Incredibly, Cathy's dear friend offered to drive her truck across the country, nearly 2,500 miles one way. So she purposed to fix her eyes not on what is seen, the miles, but on what is unseen, since what she could see with her eyes is temporary, but what she cannot see is eternal (see 2 Corinthians 4:18).

Cathy recounted how she and her friend started the trip in high spirits. Soon though, as the trip progressed, they realized how far 2,500 miles really is. Cathy's health began to wane and her vomiting increased with each passing mile. Despite this, she knew she had been called by Jesus to sojourn to the ranch and refused to let severe illness stop her.

Every time they considered turning back, the Lord said, quoting Isaiah 41:10, *"Do not fear [anything], for I am with you; do not be afraid, for I am your God. I will strengthen you, be assured I will help you; I will certainly take hold of you with My righteous right hand"* (AMP). So they persevered and kept pressing into what felt more impossible every day.

Each mile became more difficult as Cathy's illness escalated. Yet she clung to the Lord for strength when they despaired of ever reaching Oregon. And the power of Jesus' words became her lifeline: "This sickness is not unto death, but for the glory of God, that the Son of God may be glorified through it" (John 11:4 NKJV).

By God's grace alone, six and a half days later they reached Crystal Peaks fifteen minutes before the start of the conference.

When I met Cathy, it was obvious that she was indeed very ill. Often, when I checked in with her throughout the clinic, I found her either sitting flat on the barn floor or on the ranch grass. Clinging to the ground seemed to be the only place where her nausea was held at bay.

Yet as intense as her symptoms were, and even though her pallor matched the green grass upon which she often sat, she was always smiling. Even between jags of vomiting, she continued to exude a strong spirit of joy.

I was moved by her tenacious persistence to choose gladness despite her obvious hardships. Through her suffering, she never lost sight of Jesus. She saw Him cut a swathe through her ocean of distance and she was going to take one faithful step after another . . . following where He wanted her to go.

During the clinic, my prayer over her swirled. *Jesus, meet her here in a way that she knows it's You. Fulfill her eager expectation of experiencing You in this place. Reveal the power of Your love for her.*

Day after day, she lavished me with one brilliant smile after another. Beyond all the Spirit-led teachings and how-to classes, she delighted in sharing her most important takeaway from the clinic, above all else, that her life was not about her. God was calling Cathy to something far greater than herself, and she could not do any of it without Him. Still beaming, she related how she sensed Crystal Peaks was "a very God-honoring, special place, where the power, grace and faithfulness of the Lord are on full display."

I could not help but smile back into her radiant face. She had verbalized exactly what I was thinking about her.

As is our private way, several on our staff chose to fast and pray over the participants before they arrived. Among them arose a common desire: "We can gather together and pray over Cathy." Indeed, we could pray over her. But I sensed the Holy Spirit was giving more time for her to choose what she wanted. By allowing her time to ask for prayer, her heart would reflect the same belief as the woman who pushed through the crowd to touch Jesus (see Mark 5:27). Her faith was so aligned with the heart of her Father that she knew if she could touch the Son, she would be healed.

Partly because of her respect for others' needs before her own, Cathy's request for prayer did come—moments before the clinic commissioning on the last day. Judy, my beloved friend, faithful assistant and prayer warrior pulled me aside with the news.

In a matter of minutes, I placed Cathy's walker in the back of a Ranger. She, Judy and I all slid in and carefully drove up as high on the ranch as possible. We all wanted to be as close as we could safely move her to the cross, which stands on the highest point of the property.

In this sacred place, our prayer started as pure worship of the One who is worthy. During this trio of prayerful worship, the Spirit showed me an image of something that looked like a campfire in the darkness. Every time a breeze blew across it, a hail of sparks showered through Cathy's heart, each leaving an equal number of trailing scorch marks. I asked my friend what she thought this "fire" might represent.

She started to weep. "I know what that fire is." She paused. "It's fear."

When given the choice of chasing the sparks or going after the fire of her fear, my brave friend walked straight into the inferno.

Waging war through prayer, she spoke out every fear-producing lie the enemy had used to confine her in a prison of anxiety. Firmly rebuking each with the name of Jesus and the blood of Jesus, she stamped out the blaze with her own feet. Feet that had always been free. Beautiful feet not created to stand idle, shackled in fear, but to move forward in bearing the Gospel of Jesus' love.

All the lies and fears she had learned to live with were destroyed in a single encounter with the living God. She recognized latent anxiety had been part of her life for so long that its black poison had infected her well-being, health and relationships in damaging ways.

As Cathy pressed deeper into the place where her war was being waged, we all slid out of the Ranger and moved to the front, where we could easily stand while leaning back on the bumper. In this position, she continued to forcefully stamp her feet in hearty agreement with the trouncing of the enemy's lies within her soul.

In rapid succession, she called out every deception that had stolen from her life and imprisoned her peace. One by one, she made them all bow before the truth of God's Word. Now exposed to the infinite brilliance of His presence, each one incinerated within the true, holy fire that is Him (see Hebrews 12:29).

In turn, His white-hot freedom ignited her soul with equal speed.

Her overwhelming gratitude could not be contained in mere words. With her eyes closed and her face tipped toward the heavens, she reached her hands skyward. A steady stream of tears kept pace with the steady stream of praise pouring from her lips, as if to sluice away the black sludge of oppression that had long been her constant companion.

Today was eviction day for all that once held her captive in fear. Because of what Jesus has done and made available for all, she emptied her hands and heart of all fear, only to take the hand of the One who has conquered all fear. Indeed, it started to rain. Great drops of freedom poured over us all. Within this moment, the Lord wanted me to see how release washed in gratitude could galvanize into raw faith. This daughter of the King was dancing with eyes closed, hands raised in pure gratitude before the One who purchased her freedom. And that is when I noticed something beyond beautiful. The same woman with severe vertigo, the same woman who was forced to move with a walker and sit on the ground to quench her violent vomiting attacks, the same woman who moments earlier believed the power of her fear was greater than the power of her God . . . was dancing. This *was* the same woman, my sister in Christ who before my eyes exchanged clinging to the ground to clinging to Jesus.

Now mine were the eyes flooding with gratitude.

The moment that followed will remain etched in my heart forever. Quietly, I called to the newly released woman at my side, "Cathy, Cathy, my friend."

Clearly not wanting to break the moment, she glanced at me over the top of her arm, with her hands still raised in the air.

"Cathy, you've been dancing in worship with your eyes closed and your arms up for the last fifteen minutes . . . without holding on to anything. Friend, Jesus has done more than heal your heart, He's healed your body, too. It's time to receive this healing, inside and out, from the One who loves you most."

Cathy's elbows dropped slightly as realization of all that He had done poured into her heart. Her momentary expression of puzzling the pieces together was suddenly overwhelmed by a wave of pure joy. Her eyes and smile met in the middle to make one of the greatest expressions of gratitude I have ever seen.

Together, we all made our way up the steep incline to the cross. Falling to our knees, we gave praise and thanksgiving to the One who gives freedom to anyone who *asks* and keeps asking—and believes and keeps believing.

After our time of adoration was complete, we all slowly rose to our feet.

"And now it's time," I said, looking into her dancing eyes, "to give glory to Jesus."

Far below us down in the ranch main yard, Troy, my husband, had already begun to commission the rest of the assembly. I offered to give Cathy a ride down the steep hill.

With her trademark glittering smile, she declined in favor of walking with Jesus. She wanted to immediately strengthen her new stance in Him.

So I tossed her walker in the back of the Ranger and headed toward the gathering below. As I drove, realization poured into my heart: Our faith does not exist in any heart . . . until we walk in it.

After parking behind the gathering, I jogged the short distance to rejoin Troy, who was leading the group. Suddenly, the friend who spent six and a half days of her life driving Cathy to the ranch stood up and stared at me over the crowd, as if to ask, *Where's my friend?*

I smiled and mutely pointed up the gravel road that led to the back of the ranch.

She turned to see Cathy, walking unassisted, down from the cross. Cathy's faithful friend screamed, and her knees started to buckle. She caught herself and instantly started to run toward her once-ailing sister. Together, in the middle of the gravel road, they collided in a tearful, enduring, crumpled embrace.

"In his kindness God called you to share in his eternal glory by means of Christ Jesus. So after you have suffered a little while, he will restore, support, and strengthen you, and he will place you on a firm foundation" (1 Peter 5:10).

Cathy's foundation was so firm that she left her walker at Crystal Peaks next to the trash can. She tossed all her medication as well.

Later, she documented her encounter with Jesus and sent it to me. She shared that it was hard at first to stand in her new faith and believe. But Jesus reminded her of His Word in John 10:10: "The thief's purpose is to steal and kill and destroy. My purpose is to give them a rich and satisfying life."

She wrote:

We left Crystal Peaks for the long road home playing loud worship music and singing praises to the Lord. Our great adventure was over, but what a testimony to the Lord's greatness, mercy, provision and faithfulness. What an experience in learning that God's leading is sometimes hard and costly, but is always worth it.

Cathy had faith. She believed that faith is the confidence that what we hope for will actually happen; it gives us assurance about things we cannot see (see Hebrews 11:1).

When she sensed her God drawing her from afar, she had faith to go. "It was by faith that Abraham obeyed when God called him to leave home and go to another land that God would give him as his inheritance" (v. 8).

She had faith in not only knowing the Word of God; she believed His Word because "faith comes from hearing, that is, hearing the Good News about Christ" (Romans 10:17).

When she fell desperately ill and was told by medical professionals that the journey was impossible, she had faith to still believe. Her faith did "not rest in the wisdom of men but in the power of God" (1 Corinthians 2:5 ESV).

When she was miserable during the journey, she had faith and pressed on. "I consider that our present sufferings are not worth comparing with the glory that will be revealed in us" (Romans 8:18 NIV).

When she had to sit on the ground for most of a week, she had faith to choose joy. "Dear brothers and sisters, when troubles . . . come your way, consider it an opportunity for great joy. For you know that when your faith is tested, your endurance has a chance to grow" (James 1:2–3).

When she was driven up to the cross to pray, she had faith that the Lord would meet her. "I prayed to the LORD, and he answered me. He freed me from all my fears. . . . In my desperation I prayed, and the LORD listened; he saved me from all my troubles" (Psalm 34:4–6).

When she stood face-to-face in His presence in worship, because of her faith He healed her completely. "O LORD, if you heal me, I will be truly healed; if you save me, I will be truly saved. My praises are for you alone!" (Jeremiah 17:14).

Not at any point was Cathy walking by sight, her every step was guided by her unshakable faith. And because of her faith, Jesus met her in a powerful, life-changing, unforgettable way.

Most believers know a zillion verses about faith. We adorn our walls with them, read them to our kids and quote them to our friends. But few actually believe these verses enough to apply them.

The Old Testament records that the Red Sea was parted (see Exodus 14:15–31), the sky was shut (see 1 Kings 17:1), the sun held fast (see Joshua 10:12–13), lions' mouths were closed (see Daniel 6:22) and armies were routed (see 2 Chronicles 20). In the New Testament, as well, we see a beautiful faith-inspiring pattern: diseases cured, demons cast out, the dead raised and sin defeated.

When God poured His healing power through Jesus, the disciples, the apostles or believers, often the one receiving the gift was encouraged to do something they could not do before.

The recipient of God's power was asked to do the previously difficult or impossible, such as stand and walk (see Acts 3), go and wash in a pool when you are still blind (see John 9), go into the temple and show yourself to the priests when you still have advanced leprosy (see Luke 17).

None of these were healed when they set out on their faith walk. Rather, they were healed *during* their journey because, by faith, they believed God and did what they were asked to do. None of them saw the miracle first. All of them experienced the miracle once they took individual actions of faith. Indeed, for each of us, seeing is not believing, for "we live by believing and not by seeing" (2 Corinthians 5:7).

Throughout my life, I have come to realize this truth: Fear in response to survival will keep you alive; fear by itself will keep you in prison. But faith in God releases His power into our circumstances. Simply knowing this should make us jump up and down and cheer. Yet we do not cheer. What stops us from pursuing an all-powerful gift that transforms our life, our world and the atmospheres we inhabit?

Pride.

We trust our pride, what we think we know, more than the truth and power of God's Word. When we get stuck in this posture, we reflect the religious leaders of Jesus' day. They all knew God's Word; they just did not believe it. Had they believed what they knew, their hearts would have been transformed. Other than when Jesus cleared the temple, the sharpest arrows of His anger were aimed at these.

Throughout the gospels, the religious leaders persisted in challenging Jesus to "perform" a miraculous sign. With arms folded across their chests, they demanded He prove Himself. Their focus was locked on discrediting Him instead of the condition of their own heart. Had they simply believed *Him*, they would not have needed a sign, because God would have poured His miraculous love through *them*.

From God, are you demanding a sign—or believing for one?

Genuine faith does not sit on the couch and complain. Genuine faith draws us forward into action. Often it beckons us into directions that do not make sense. But if we listen to the voice of His Spirit, we hear Him calling, *Will you trust Me more than your logic? More than your understanding? More than your education? More than your skill set? More than your experience? More than your emotion? Will you trust Me more than you?*

This is the realm where faith is forged.

Jesus Himself said in Mark 16:15–20 that "these miraculous signs will accompany those who believe": They will cast out demons, speak new languages, handle external dangers safely, handle internal dangers safely and heal the sick.

Jesus determined these five attributes will accompany those who believe. Are they present in you? If not, why not? What is blocking you from a life hallmarked by the signs that Jesus states should accompany all believers?

We can justify our faith in any way we choose. But James chapter 2 is clear: Faith without action is dead; it is not faith at all. And unfortunately, without faith, it is impossible to please God (see Hebrews 11:6).

Our focus should not be centered on *if* God can still do the miraculous (read His Word—He can). Our focus should be riveted on what is so broken within our own faith that the flow of His presence is quenched by our unbelief.

The revival of our faith is not something that we see and then accept. It is something we believe, and then, like Cathy and the saints in Hebrews chapter 11, we walk forward with eager expectation that His Word, His promises will come alive in us.

When we trust in God more than our fear, more than our pride, more than our complacency, more than us—this is the glorious fire in which our faith is restored.

Jesus, this is the realm I choose to pursue. The realm beyond my human selfishness, understanding and control. I choose to pursue the realm where You are. Because it is in this place that You proclaim, "Nothing is impossible with God!" (Luke 1:37 TPT).

May nothing be impossible through this vessel.

My beautiful Savior,

Right now, I give You my spiritual vertigo, my sorry need to cling to what I know.

I don't want to be faithless any longer. I choose to not waste another minute of this precious life stuck in my prison of fear.

By obeying my fear I'm rejecting Your truth—and the joy, freedom and purpose it brings.

Today, I'm walking away from all fake religion and propped-up-with-cardboard faith.

Jesus, I release my prideful need to control the outcome. Show me the awful source of my fear that is quenching my faith, Lord. I give all my fear to You.

I choose to stop embracing the ground—and start embracing my God. My faith will only become real when I trust You enough to walk in it.

Today is that day.

I'm leaving my dungeon of fear . . . and walking into Your rich and satisfying life. Because nothing is impossible for You and Your Spirit lives in me, nothing will be impossible through this vessel either.

Today, my beloved Savior, I release my fear—all of it—and embrace Your faith.

Amen.

SIX

Restore My Worship

*Jesus, please restore my passionate
desire to worship You alone.*

I will praise the LORD all my life; I will sing praise to my
God as long as I live.

Psalm 146:2 NIV

My phone buzzed. I was delighted to see it was my beloved
husband, Troy. Upon answering, I noticed his usual up-
beat tone was cloaked with heavy concern. "I'm in a meeting
with two of our staff," he said. "It's not good. You need to
come down to my office and hear this for yourself."

It was August, the month of my birth. I was born on the
nineteenth, the number in Scripture that symbolizes faith. Yet
in this moment, my faith was not in the fact that my husband
was a very good actor. I was certain this was the beginning of
a birthday ambush, and once outside I would be waylaid by
my staff and tossed headfirst into the nearest horse trough.

With my senses on high alert, I opened my front door. Cautiously, I walked down the hill onto the ranch main yard. Many

staff were scattered throughout the area and appeared busy with their daily tasks. None seemed to notice my passage toward Troy's office.

Hmm, maybe their acting skills have improved. Quietly, respectfully, I pushed open his office door and was instantly affronted by a heavy pale of oppression that filled the room. One look at my husband's ashen face told me this was no joke, birthday or any other.

Troy's words fell flat. "You'd better sit down."

The report that poured from our staff was a retelling of many conversations from a beloved soul who had been coming to the ranch for nearly a decade. The tale recounted personal wounds that had been collected through the years. Like slivers, small misunderstandings, which would have been simple to clarify in the moment, were instead left to fester. Over the years, these minor slivers had matured into ugly boils of mistrust and anger, buoyed by a record of wrongs and pride.

The allegations leveled against the ranch grew into a savage monster that rotated and stared down directly at me. Hurled like angry rocks, these infected criticisms were not shot at the ranch operations—but at me personally. The crosshairs of accusation were aimed at my integrity, purpose, ministry and relationship with my King.

After enduring this verbal stoning for over an hour, I walked back up the hill. My legs would hardly move; they felt like concrete. My heart was so heavy, so intensely sad. I loved this individual, the family's children were precious to me and now all were going to be swept away from the ranch—blameless casualties of adult bitterness.

My heart broke for these innocents who were being stripped away from a place they loved, a place they felt safe. Because of pride, I would not see them again. Indeed, minor mistakes *had* been made—but nothing a simple exchange of clarity could not have resolved in minutes of honest conversation.

Grappling with what felt like multiple bullet holes in my chest, I examined my heart. *Jesus, show me my part of this and how to make it right before You. Burn away the emotion and speak Your truth into this situation. Show me what You desire.*

I opened the door of my home and barely made it into my office. I slumped into my chair. Welling tears of grief could wait no longer. Leaning forward, my elbows fell onto the desktop as my head dropped in my hands. Droplets of sadness, loss, remorse and exhaustion dotted the old barn wood of my desk.

I cried over the hearts that had been wounded.

I cried over the innocent children I would never see again.

I cried until my head ached nearly as much as my heart.

I cried until there were no more tears, just empty sorrow.

Then, in this dark place, something like an old Persian rug appeared all around me. In my mind the rug was heavy and deep red in hue, the color of dried blood. And it was filthy, with a smell more hideous than its grimy presence. Upon it flowed creamy damp rivulets that looked exactly like . . . flowing pus. This awful carpet was on top of me.

With my head still in my hands, I breathed, "Jesus, what do You want me to do?"

His answer was instant and simple.

I want you to worship Me . . . right now.

Inhaling deeply, I slowly moved my upturned palms away from my face and began to speak whispered praise to my Savior. Words, cracked with emotion, strung together to form a simple song of worship. As I sang, the deathly, stinking carpet over me began to curl up from its edges toward its center. The more I spoke adoration to Jesus, the higher my hands lifted. The higher my hands rose, the stronger my heart felt. The more I spoke my love for Jesus, the more the horrible carpet retreated. Finally, in a flourish of praise, I shot up to my feet with my hands lifted high in the air.

In that instant, the carpet of oppression recoiled, as if shrinking away from its own destruction. Caught in shrunken retreat, its moorings were loosened. Then, the mighty wind of the Holy Spirit rushed in and blew it off me.

Walls could not contain the outpouring of love and gratitude rising skyward from a redeemed girl to her beloved King. And I saw this truth: Genuine worship of Jesus through any situation is one of the mightiest weapons of spiritual warfare a believer has, because the enemy has no defense against it.

When we choose praise within our pain, we are telling our enemy that we do not fear him. Instead, we fear Jesus—and He is crazy about us.

Praise in our pain crushes the enemy because it is a response, an outpouring of the Holy Spirit. And our enemy has no authority over the Spirit of the living God. So when we respond in the Spirit by praising Jesus, Satan is completely defeated. His tactics of mixed truths, lies and hyperfocus on what hurts are destroyed when we reach through the black vortex of his confusion and lift our hands in adoration to the One who is the same yesterday, today and forever.

Jesus is our Rock that never rolls. When we reestablish our hope in Him, we will not be shaken either.

Worship was never meant to be about our comfort. It is not about comfy chairs and the right songs or leaders. In Jonah chapters 1–2, the people of Nineveh, when confronted with their sin, repented and turned from their junk and toward God. Then they gave God a sacrifice of praise.

A sacrifice is releasing something that has value to us, something that costs us personally. Praise is meant to be alive. It is meant to cost us something—our pride, our fear, our complacency, our comfort, our bitterness and our doubt. We worship to give a gift to the One who is worthy.

Through worship, focus, purpose and peace were restored—genuine praise does that.

"Now, who will want to harm you if you are eager to do good? But even if you suffer for doing what is right, God will reward you for it. So *don't worry or be afraid of their threats. Instead, you must worship Christ as Lord of your life*" (1 Peter 3:13–15, emphasis added).

When our focus shifts toward our great big problems, and lingers there, our perspective of God gets smaller and smaller, shrinking in direct proportion to the duration of our downward attention. While looking at what lies below, it is perilously easy to fall headfirst into the black well of pessimism. Instead of bringing life, our words become a negative gush, flowing unrestrained through black culverts that spew the putrid sewage of our gloomy circumstances to anyone who will listen.

When our focus gets jammed in this downward position, Satan laughs. Why? Because he has seduced one more child of God to glorify his evil work.

Complaining is the telltale sewage leak of a heart that is so backed up with a continual focus on pain—for weeks, months, years, decades—that negativity is the overflow. Jesus said, "Whatever is in your heart determines what you say" (Matthew 12:34). Our words, our countenance, our actions give evidence of what fills our hearts.

When our focus rests on our great big God in worship, our troubles minimize in perspective and comparison to His almighty presence. We will still have troubles. But they do not have us—unless we give them authority to move into our heart. We can walk through hardships with our face tipped upward in perpetual worship of the One who is worthy. When locked in this posture, we become an unstoppable glittering waterfall of life that gushes His glorious radiance into the world around us. The overflow of a heart filled with His goodness continually testifies of what *He* has done—and can do in any heart who adores Him through hard circumstances.

Through worship, we become a conduit for the voice of the Spirit of heaven. The more we speak of His glory, the more His glory and His very presence fills us, the more we become like Him.

When our focus is on Him, no matter what we face, we can have peace. And in that peace, there is freedom.

The apostle Peter reminds us of this:

> Dear friends, don't be surprised at the fiery trials you are going through, as if something strange were happening to you. Instead, be very glad—for these trials make you partners with Christ in his suffering, so that you will have the wonderful joy of seeing his glory when it is revealed to all the world.
>
> If you are insulted because you bear the name of Christ, you will be blessed, *for the glorious Spirit of God rests upon you.*
>
> 1 Peter 4:12–14, emphasis added

If rejoicing in Jesus through suffering draws His Spirit to rest upon me, *that* is pain worth having.

Paul and Silas knew this truth. In Acts 16, they were falsely accused, stripped naked in public, beaten nearly to death, then thrown into the deepest, darkest dungeon in the land and put in stocks—for doing nothing wrong. From the world's perspective, they had every right to cry out, *God, why? Why? Why?* But they never wavered. They kept their eye on the prize and chose to not blame God . . . but worship Him.

It was their worship that invited the Spirit of the living God into their circumstances. And when the Holy Spirit entered into their place of pain, He shook loose their bondage, and the enemy's attack was instantly defeated. Through worship, everyone present was flooded with the life-giving presence of Jesus, and they all received His redemption.

Worship breaks off the enemy's attack.

More proof of this truth is found in 2 Chronicles 20. King Jehoshaphat and the entire nation of Judah were about to be annihilated by not one, not two, but three armies so vast they could not be counted. The terrified king's instant response was to order his entire kingdom to join him in seeking the Lord through fasting and prayer.

The Lord answered and gave this counsel: "Do not be afraid! Don't be discouraged by this mighty army, for the battle is not yours, but God's. . . . You will not even need to fight. Take your positions; then stand still and watch the LORD's victory. He is with you" (vv. 15, 17).

Now notice what happened next:

> The king appointed singers to walk ahead of the army, singing to the LORD and praising him for his holy splendor. This is what they sang: "Give thanks to the LORD; his faithful love endures forever!" At the very moment they began to sing and give praise, the LORD caused the armies of Ammon, Moab, and Mount Seir to start fighting among themselves. . . . They began attacking each other. . . . Not a single one of the enemy had escaped.
>
> vv. 21–24

Again, worship broke off the enemy's attack.

God's people did not retaliate, fight back or self-justify. They simply turned to God and worshiped Him.

"Therefore, let us offer through Jesus a *continual sacrifice of praise* to God, proclaiming our allegiance to his name" (Hebrews 13:15, emphasis added).

Friend, we know we will suffer. We know the Lord calls us to be ready. And we know when hardships toss a rotten layer of heartache over us, we have a choice to make. We can choose to focus on the pain and be filled with sorrow, left to languish under a putrid covering of oppression. Or we can choose to focus on the unbreakable promises of our God and be filled with His gladness and blanketed by His glorious Spirit.

We choose.

"We were crushed and overwhelmed beyond our ability to endure, and we thought we would never live through it. In fact, we expected to die. But as a result, *we stopped relying on ourselves and learned to rely only on God*, who raises the dead" (2 Corinthians 1:8–9, emphasis added).

Notice again the verse, "We stopped relying on ourselves and learned to rely on God." Is not our hardship worth that? Is not learning to trust wholeheartedly on God worth some heartache, especially when that heartache draws His Spirit to rest upon us?

The enemy is only empowered in our life when we choose to agree with his lies, his deceptions, his twisting of God's truths to bend us away from the Author of truth.

I have seen the awful carpet since that day. But now I know what oppression looks like and how easy it is to defeat. Now I recognize the choice between worry or worship—deflation in my junk or elation in my God.

His Word says, "Rejoice in the Lord always. Again I will say, rejoice!" (Philippians 4:4 NKJV). "This is the day the LORD has made. We will rejoice and be glad in it" (Psalm 118:24). And, "I heard what sounded like a great multitude . . . shouting: 'Hallelujah! For our Lord God Almighty reigns. Let us rejoice and be glad and give him glory!'" (Revelation 19:6–7 NIV).

God calls us to praise Him not only when it is easy but even, and especially, when it is hard.

Life is filled with hardships; they pave a road each of us must walk. But our choice to praise God will honor Him and give us joy in the journey. It will draw the glorious Spirit of our God to rest upon us.

"Your unfailing love is better than life itself; how I praise you!" David wrote in Psalm 63:3. "I will praise you as long as I live, lifting up my hands to you in prayer. You satisfy me more than the richest feast. I will praise you with songs of joy" (vv. 4–5).

Lord Jesus,
   Today I step into that holy place, the transforming fire that is worship of You, my King.
   Whatever I choose to focus on has the power to fill and lead my life. I must choose between my great big problems—or my great big God! I cannot look backward and forward at the same time. I can only go one way. I can only move in the direction of my focus.
   Jesus, You did not *die on the cross so I could remain living with my head stuck in a position of looking downward at my pain.*
   Today, I choose to look upward and focus on You above whatever might trouble me. I acknowledge that praising You does not make my problems go away—it makes my self-imposed oppression go away. When I choose to delight in You during my hardships, I receive Your joy for the journey and this beautiful exaltation draws Your glorious Spirit to rest upon me.
   Your Spirit resting on me.
   Your Word calls me to "consider it all joy" when I encounter hardships because they are the necessary fuel that grows my endurance (James 1:2 NASB). And when my endurance is fully mature, I will be "perfect and complete, lacking nothing" (v. 4). How can I know that verse and not run through hard days jumping and cheering at the awareness that I am being made mature and complete, lacking in no good thing?
   Jesus, thank You for walking this road with me. Thank You for showing me the way. Thank You for Your loving

presence no matter what lies ahead. Simply knowing that You are always with me is reason enough to worship You every minute of every day.

I love You.

Amen.

SEVEN

Restore My Forgiveness

Jesus, please restore my honest desire to forgive.

"Our Father in heaven, . . . forgive us our sins, as we have forgiven those who sin against us."

Matthew 6:9, 12

The long-awaited day of August 21 had finally arrived. The anticipation was so great that over one million visitors from all over the world crushed into the center portion of our state to view this rare phenomenon.

Central Oregon was in the path of a total solar eclipse.

The local roads were expected to be so choked with traffic that a normal fifteen-minute commute would be transformed into hours of gridlock. Not really knowing what to expect, my husband, Troy, and I made the decision to close the ranch on this day.

As if preparing for the Big Game, Troy hauled out one of our old rocking chairs into the middle of the yard. Next, he donned a pair of stylish "eclipse glasses" given to us by a dear friend. Clearly, they were designed for eye protection only. The glasses' boxy paper-and-plastic design made him look more as if he was expecting an alien landing.

Taking his seat in the center of the lawn, he was ready for the big show.

The world watched as the moon eased its way closer toward intercepting the path of the sun. Contact was made as the rim of the moon edged over our perpetual source of light. At first, there was no discernable change. The raw power of light was not minimized by the encroaching veil of the moon. But over time, a strangeness filled the air. As if on a gradual dimmer switch, moment by moment, the light lessened. Had one not been looking for the loss, it would have been easy to miss.

I was awed that even when the sun was seventy percent covered, it still produced so much power that there was little difference in what earth experienced. I was also aware of when light changes slowly, our eyes adjust accordingly—virtually making our environment appear unchanged. Finally, as ninety percent was eclipsed, an eerie half-light covered the land. The animals lay down. The chickens gathered in the coop to roost. The birds stopped flying. All sound stopped. The air was still.

I wondered if this was what it looked like as Jesus chose to acquire, forgive and destroy each of our sins as He hung on the cross.

Then, totality. The sun was completely covered. One hundred percent of its life-giving presence was blocked by the celestial body of the moon. It was 10:30 a.m.

Darkness fell across the land. My first impression was that it felt like . . . grief.

It seemed as if the earth were literally mourning the loss of the one appointed to give life. Although I expected the darkness, something else happened that was completely unexpected.

Cold.

In seconds, literally seconds, the temperature took a noticeable plunge. A disconcerting chill covered the land. On this otherwise hot August day, my arms responded to the instant shift with unnatural, unnerving goose bumps.

A primal angst rose within. Every cell rocked into heightened awareness. There was a silent alarm, *This isn't right!* Without conscious direction, a single desire erupted from every DNA strand inside my body. An urgent, unified chorus rang out, *I want the sun back!*

From our region, totality lasted less than a minute. Yet in one minute—one single minute without the sun—darkness and cold reigned.

As the moon continued its ordered course, a narrow sliver of the opposite side of the sun reemerged. A blast of light cut through the chill of darkness. Instantaneously, both darkness and cold were incinerated by the glory of its unstoppable force.

As the visual "dimmer switch" reversed, the birds started to sing their glorious morning song, announcing a new day. The chickens emerged from the coop. The ranch animals got back to their feet and stretched. And life went on . . . as if the planetary blackout had never happened.

Lying in bed that same night, I asked the Holy Spirit to speak into this extraordinary experience. *Please help me understand what I saw. And even more . . . what I felt.*

The answer did not come right away. In fact, it did not come for nearly a year. But when it did, it was simply this:

Forgiveness.

I had just experienced the fallout of the most challenging season of deception, accusation and betrayal I have ever known. Apparently, this was needed to fully understand the true depth of what He wanted me to learn—and *apply.*

As if wading through a putrid flood, no matter where I went, who I was with or how much I tried to focus on other things, the stench of what surrounded me was ever present. It filled my thoughts, it tainted my words, it infiltrated my actions. Even my dreams were invaded by the black swirl. Over time, it consumed the bandwidth of my focus. My every effort to give grace, to trust conversations, to hope my perceptions were incorrect were all slowly drowned beneath the rising tide of my own unforgiveness.

This I know of the vessel in which I live: I am not ruffled by much. My heart is simple and my head straightforward. I believe the best in the words and actions of those around me. I am not easily offended. This might sound admirable so far.

But the nasty underbelly of my humanity is that once I embrace offense, it can take me nearly as long to walk it out and let it go. This is not a justification by any stretch. In fact, it is the opposite. It is a life-sized mirror that reflects the pure ugliness of choosing to "take offense." In any form, unforgiveness is simply not okay.

And even worse, it separates my heart from God's heart. And what offense could possibly be worth that?

During the eclipse, I noticed the slow fade of light. I witnessed the glory of the sun being obstructed. I experienced the surreal cold of when its presence is blocked. *This* is what unforgiveness does between our hearts and God's.

My decision to allow unforgiveness to take up residence in my life literally blocks the Father's glory from shining on, in or through my life. It was never God's decision that I choose to live in self-appointed darkness any more than He would choose for the world to live in perpetual solar eclipse.

When my heart is overshadowed by unforgiveness, God is not responsible—I am.

It is a true statement, "Bitterness rots the container that holds it."

Think about what it truly means to "harbor" unforgiveness in your heart. A harbor is a place of safety, a place where we store what is most valuable to us to protect it from storm damage. When we choose to drive bitterness into the harbor of our hearts and tie it up right next to all we hold dear, including our relationship with Jesus, we expose the most precious parts of who we are to this invasive rot.

"People who conceal their sins will not prosper, but if they confess and turn from them, they will receive mercy" (Proverbs 28:13).

I did not realize that I was concealing sin in the harbor of my heart. The dimming of His glory happened so gradually that I did not recognize I had adjusted to being content with a sliver of His life-giving light. I had gotten used to the silent alarm that alerted, *This isn't right!*

No wonder God does not *ask* us to forgive; He commands us to. "Be kind to each other, tenderhearted, forgiving one another, just as God through Christ has forgiven you" (Ephesians 4:32). And, "if you refuse to forgive others, your Father will not forgive your sins" (Matthew 6:15).

By choosing not to forgive, I was telling God that I loved my stance of self-justification more than Him. By refusing God's command, I had inadvertently established me as the god of my heart.

Ouch!

The truth is this: Forgiveness has nothing to do with what has been done against us; it has everything to do with what we are doing about our heart condition before God.

Revival cannot happen within me while I am approaching God unapologetically with unforgiveness in my heart. Before God, this must look like me coming into His presence while dragging a dead body behind me, and then having the audacity to ask *Him, What stinks in here?*

Unforgiveness is a deadly sin that no human façade can hide. It is chained to the pit of hell, and our destruction is its singular hideous goal. For anyone who wants to live in hell on earth, choose to not forgive someone—and you will get there instantly.

Yet for such a formidable foe, because of what Jesus did on the cross for each of us, He has placed the key in my hand. How dare I stand before God and others and self-justify that I have been wronged when Jesus, by giving His life, has already given me the key to forgive.

"If we *claim we have no sin, we are only fooling ourselves* and not living in the truth. But if we *confess our sins to him*, he is faithful and just to forgive us our sins and to cleanse us from all wickedness" (1 John 1:8–9, emphasis added).

As previously mentioned, this I know: Not one person has ever been born with eyes on the back of his or her head. Why? Because we are not designed to habitually examine the past.

By continually looking backward, we fan a painful blaze that needs to die. This perpetual ache within is fueled by our constant choice to keep looking back at the offenses. We relive them. We tally them. We organize them like evil soldiers to support and validate our self-justification. We get used to that constant pain in our neck from being torqued around and fixated on the past, instead of "forgetting the past and looking forward to what lies ahead" (Philippians 3:13).

Genuine forgiveness cannot happen if we keep insisting on looking back at the past. Looking backward only strengthens the rotting corpse of self-justification. Nor does genuine forgiveness proceed from kicking and screaming. If our hearts are still stuck praying from the platform of, *God, make me . . . make me want to forgive . . . make me want to love . . . make me want resolution*, we are only telling God that we honestly do not want these things—or we would choose them with a heart softened by willingness. Asking God to "make us" do anything is the adult reflection of a childish heart that says, *I know I should—but I don't want to.*

Jesus desires that we choose to "want to." He did not endure the cross so we could have daily access to retreat into our pain, bitterness or unforgiveness. He did not endure the cross so our hearts could remain stony and hard.

My beloved friend Judy observes, "Why are God's people so fixated on looking backward and digging up, and redigging up, and digging through what they've already dug up? When it comes to generational sin . . . when we look backward, all we see is blame! When we purpose to look forward, all we see is His blessing! Forward in Him is where our hope is found!"

Indeed, for those who love Jesus, it is time to stop looking backward—we are not going that way.

In sharp contrast, the world proclaims, even through professionals, *You're justified to be bitter. It's okay to rage. It's healing to return to the altar of your offense. You need time to process your pain. Learn effective coping mechanisms. Set boundaries.*

We can agree with the proclamations of this world and stay locked in perpetual spiritual eclipse. Or, we can follow Jesus stride for stride into the brilliant beautiful blueprint of *true* forgiveness found in Luke 6, starting with verse 27:

"But to you who are willing to listen,

1. "Love your enemies!"
2. "Do good to those who hate you."
3. "Bless those who curse you" (v. 28).
4. "Pray for those who hurt you."
5. "Do to others as you would like them to do to you" (v. 31).

He concludes, "You must be compassionate, just as your Father is compassionate" (v. 36). This is the wisdom of Jesus. Step for hallowed, sacred step, this is Jesus' path to forgiveness. *For those "who are willing to listen"* (v. 27).

Am I willing to listen? Am I willing to love, do good, bless, pray and treat others well? Am I willing to reflect the warm, radiant compassion of my Dad? Am I willing to come to God with a soft heart, a humble heart, and be willing to listen?

True forgiveness begins when we choose to stop complaining and start listening. It grows when we allow our hearts to bend back toward humility.

> Do not bring sorrow to God's Holy Spirit by the way you live . . . Get rid of all *bitterness, rage, anger, harsh words, and slander,* as well as all types of evil behavior. Instead, be kind to each other, tenderhearted, *forgiving one another, just as God through Christ has forgiven you.*
>
> Ephesians 4:30–32, emphasis added

Just like the solar eclipse, when we allow bitterness to accumulate in our hearts, over time this invasive plague blocks our relationship with God the Father. We know it is getting darker, but instead of fixing the problem in our hearts, we choose instead to get used to the growing darkness. The colder it gets, the more layers of self-justification we put on, and the more our hearts sink into the self-appointed pit of victimization. Day after week after month after year, when we continue to justify our pain as the fault of others—we do not have to change. We just get to sit in the gathering darkness.

Yet no matter how dark and cold our world gets in the eclipse of our bitterness, a voice rises from within, deep calling out to deep, *I want the sun back! I want the brilliant, molten love of my Father to drench my heart again.*

Beloved, when it comes to the restoration of your desire to forgive, in every disagreement, in every battle, in every war, the love of God always wins.

And when we repent of our sin, our faults, our wrecks, our unforgiveness—then times of refreshing will come from the presence of the Lord. If you want more of His presence, forgive now.

> Make allowance for each other's faults, and *forgive anyone who offends you.* Remember, the Lord forgave you, so you must forgive others. Above all, clothe yourselves with love, which binds us all together in perfect harmony. And *let the peace that comes from Christ rule in your hearts.*
>
> Colossians 3:13–15, emphasis added

My beloved friend Katie says, "I want to lean into the flesh-melting glory of God." Indeed, it is time to allow His glory to melt away all that shields His presence from our hearts.

When we choose to forgive those who offend us, we trade in our smelly coat of bitterness and instead clothe ourselves with the beauty of Christ's love. Only then will His peace, not our darkness, rule within our hearts.

By placing our feet into the footprints Jesus left, no eclipse of pain can withstand the inferno of the Father's love, which incinerates the darkness with pure light. Like the father running toward the Prodigal Son in Luke 15, God Himself runs to meet His beloved—His child who has come home at last.

Do not allow your pain to waste His miracle of love for you, in you, through you. Instead, it is time to let it go!

Jesus defeated sin and death so that we could do the same. Period.

This is the beautiful journey back into the radiant glory of our God. This is the journey of forgiveness.

Precious Lord,

I cannot read the power of Your Word and continue standing in my selfish justification.

I choose to no longer live in the eclipse of my unforgiveness—separated from You by my sin. You have willingly forgiven me of so much. Now I willingly come to You to forgive much.

Right now, I give You everything in my heart that wants to keep holding on to offense. I name them before Your holy presence. I give it all to You.

Jesus, fill this void in my heart with the fullness of Your love for each of those I've held hostage within. Open my eyes to see their beauty as You do.

From this day forward, every time my heart pangs with an old wound, this will be my signal to pray over them Your very best—and I will keep praying over them until my heart rests in their presence . . . and in Yours.

From this day forward, I choose to follow Your beautiful steps and LOVE, DO GOOD, BLESS, PRAY, TREAT WELL those who have harmed my life. I acknowledge they're Your sons and daughters . . . and I choose to see them through the veil of Your love.

Jesus, right now, with a heart resting in Your peace, I choose to leave my hurt behind and walk into the flesh-melting glory of Your presence.

Amen.

RENEW MY MIND

Jesus replied, "The most important commandment is this: 'Listen, O Israel! The LORD our God is the one and only LORD. And you must love the LORD your God with all your heart, all your soul, all your *mind* . . .'"

Mark 12:29–30, emphasis added

EIGHT

Renew My Obedience

*Jesus, I choose to renew my obedience to
You, Your Word, Your voice by doing what
You ask—simply because I love You.*

"So why do you keep calling me 'Lord, Lord!' when you
don't do what I say?"

Luke 6:46

t was the beginning of a new year. As He often does, the Lord
asked me to pursue Him through fasting and prayer. Other
than liquids, no food was to pass my lips until I sensed His
release. During this fast, I was also working on some highly
time-sensitive material. As only the Lord could have arranged,
an opportunity for me to stay alone on the Southern Oregon
coast became available.

I knew this time was set apart by Him—for Him. I was excited to press into this unique gift with my whole being and fully
experience all that He desired. Daily, I spent time with Him in
His Word and prayed through everything that arose within my

heart. Then came the grinding. Sitting for hours turned into days that stacked up into weeks—all to finish the job.

During this time, several resounding themes circled daily within my soul. Every morning, my prayer would start with praise and worship and roll into a singular request: *Jesus, I desire to clearly hear Your voice. Please show me the things that block my ability to harken to You fully. Reveal the blocks so I can bring each one before Your authority and make them submit, or be removed. Precious Lord, help me plainly hear the voice of Your Holy Spirit and simply obey, no matter the request.*

Another day was winding down. Desperately needing a stretch and a few supplies, I welcomed the opportunity to go to the store. Still fasting, I did not need much, so I passed the shopping carts and instead picked up a small basket. In minutes, I had everything I needed and headed toward the checkout lines. Only one was open, so I took the next position behind a man.

He appeared to be about thirty and looked as if he had lived a hard life. Yet this small coastal community supports thriving logging, cranberry and fishing industries. And because of the outdoor physical nature of any one of these jobs, many of the locals make their way home looking a bit rough. Smiling to myself, I conceded that I am married to a licensed captain and fishing guide, and I work a portion of the fall serving as his first mate and bait girl. After many a long day I, too, have stood in a grocery store line looking equally as rough as the man in front of me.

A second checker arrived and announced, "I'll take the next in line please." Although the young man was the next in line, he turned around and indicated that I take the new position. Smiling, I thanked him and moved to our left in the next line over. That is when the woman who was getting ready to check out his purchase turned around and engaged me. She was someone I had been sharing the love of Christ with during my stay.

Her expression was bright as she turned to greet me with a hug over the candy counter that separated us. While we briefly chatted, I noticed the rough-looking young man place his purchase on her counter—two ramen packets. Superseding our conversation and without missing a beat, the Holy Spirit spoke within my heart, *That's all he has. He's hungry. Help him.*

My wallet was already in my hands. Retrieving a twenty-dollar bill, I folded it up into my palm. The young man patted his pockets in the universal gesture of trying to locate finances somewhere on his body. Before I could intervene, he dashed out to a homemade camper parked in front of the door.

I asked my friend who was checking out his purchase, "Hey, does he need some money?" She shrugged and brushed off the question in a manner reflecting she deals with this scenario every day. Quickly, she returned to our conversation.

An odd angst arose in my heart: *Do I break off this conversation and run after him? My groceries are in the process of being checked with a growing line behind me. Is this young man truly in need? Would my offer offend him? Or worse, would my offer embarrass him? Or worse still, if I'm wrong, will my offer embarrass me?*

Suddenly paralyzed by an avalanche of my own questions, I did nothing when the man jogged back in, produced the change, and jogged back out with his two ramen packs. There it was, the Holy Spirit handoff. And I dropped the ball.

For this entire fast I had been begging the Spirit of the living God to speak to me clearly so I could serve Him. When the Holy Spirit asked me to step out of my comfort zone and help a man in need, my immediate response was to ask 98 questions. In six seconds flat, I flipped the entire moment to be about me instead of God, thereby telling the One I love that I care more about my pride and comfort than availing myself to Him and the one He asked me to help.

Still holding the twenty-dollar bill, I dropped my head in guilt. I had fumbled. As my drinks were being tallied, I wanted to cry. My lonely thought was, *Jesus, You still cannot trust me.* After that I thanked the checker, gathered my things and walked out the door.

The homemade camper on the little truck was gone. In my sad fog, I realized I had forgotten to buy everything on my list: shampoo, face cream and lip conditioner. Returning to the store, I rounded up the overlooked items and headed back out to my rental car.

Before stepping in, I sensed the Holy Spirit wanted me to see what He saw. I scanned the large parking lot one more time, and there it was.

Parked in the farthest away space in the southeast corner of the lot was the homemade camper. I was given another chance. I did not even stop to toss my items into the car. Praying as I walked, my request was simple: "Holy Spirit, lead me."

The young man appeared from around the back of the camper, smoking a freshly lit cigarette.

I hailed him from thirty yards away. "Hey, Brother! Did you make that camper?"

His countenance transformed from cautious to welcoming. "You bet I did!" he exclaimed, beaming with pride.

I continued to ask him many questions about his handiwork, and he delighted in showing me every detail. During our lively conversation, I noticed many bumper stickers adorning the back of his camper that were contrary to my faith.

My heart stiffened. Was I enabling negative behavior?

But my questions were cut off by His voice. *Beloved, I didn't ask you to judge him. I'm asking you to love him. He doesn't know Me yet, so his hope will be in what he does know—for now. He's still hungry . . . and I'm still asking you to help him.*

After the young man answered my questions, a slightly awkward lull hung between us. Then, he ventured, "Sometimes when I show people my camper and give them my ideas for how they can make their own . . . sometimes . . . sometimes . . . they give me a tip of gratitude. And it helps me so much."

The Holy Spirit could not have opened the door between us any wider. I wanted to laugh out loud.

Instead, I said, "Barry, thank you for sharing your camper with me. I have gotta be honest with you, the real reason I came over is to tell you something. When I saw you in the store, the Lord 'highlighted' you. Jesus wanted me to see you and to tell you that He loves you so very much. His love for you is so great that He tapped a total stranger on the shoulder and said, *Hey, see that guy? He's My son, and I love him so immeasurably more than he currently knows. To show him My love, I want you to buy him dinner. He is so precious to Me.* And so, I get to be the bearer of good news and give you this meal from the One who loves you most."

Barry tipped his head to the side, obviously trying to comprehend what poured out over his heart. His eyes filled with liquid glass. Finally, he spoke, "Are you kidding me? Wow, thank you."

I handed him the crumpled twenty and said again, "Brother, you are so mightily loved!"

Receiving the bill, he looked directly at my face and asked, "Dude, . . . can I just give you a hug?"

And there in the corner of a large parking lot in a tiny town on the Southern Oregon coast, two complete strangers embraced, bound together solely by the almighty love of God.

Still clearly at a loss for words, my new friend tried to relate the Father's love he had experienced in that moment to what he knew—universal love, energies and how all true gods are about compassion.

Again, the Holy Spirit was clear. *This is where he is right now. Don't debate him. Just remind him who I am. I will do the rest.*

So, once again, I clarified the scene. "Barry, you are so incredibly special to Jesus. He loves you so much that He asked me, a total stranger, to come and tell you how much He delights in you. His love for you is so great that He knows what you need even before you ask Him. He didn't want you to be hungry tonight, so because of His love for you, He encouraged someone to come and help you. Brother, that's powerful love! How cool is that?"

Suddenly, Barry's expression shifted. "Hey, that reminds me," he said, tapping his chin. "This is so weird. I was skateboarding over at the park. I had this super strong impression to come to this store. And I never come here 'cause it's too expensive. I knew I was supposed to wait in the parking lot. So I packed up my board and just came here . . . and then I waited . . . and then you came." Realization split his face into a beautiful smile. "And how cool is that!"

Pointing at his chest with both my hands, I declared, "*That*, my brother, is the amazing, all-powerful, all-consuming, super cool love of Jesus for *you*!"

His smile broadened even more.

"God bless you, Barry. God bless you."

He nodded in silent agreement as I backed away.

Halfway back to my car, I turned around and pointed at him again. "He loves you *so* much!" I shouted. "You, Barry!"

From across the parking lot, he shot me two giant thumbs-up.

As I slid into my car, the Holy Spirit brought even more clarity.

Beloved, you asked Me to show you the things that block your heart from hearing and following Me—I did. I allowed you to come eye to eye with your pride and feel the weight of it for a moment. Also, it was I who moved both of you outside so My son wouldn't be embarrassed. All of this, every bit of it, was an answer to your prayers.

Genuine obedience to God is beautiful. It is beautiful because it is a genuine reflection of our love for Him.

When we engage Jesus through the Holy Spirit's leadership, our obedience opens a channel between heaven and earth for the will of our heavenly Father to pour through.

Peter in Acts chapter 10 nearly mirrored how two complete strangers were both impacted by the Holy Spirit to take action. Because both were obedient, God's loving plan, for both, broke through.

Authentic revival has always been a part of God's loving plan for each of our hearts. Jesus taught this from the very beginning of His ministry. "Pray like this: Our Father in heaven, may your name be kept holy. May your Kingdom come soon. *May your will be done on earth, as it is in heaven*" (Matthew 6:9–10, emphasis added).

When we choose to live a life of obedience before our Father and obey what He asks us to do, we become living vessels that carry the will of God from heaven to earth. And when God's will impacts earth, nothing within the hearts of men can withstand the flood of His love.

Revival within any heart cannot happen if we refuse to obey the One we claim we serve.

When we refuse to obey, the ministry meant to pour through us will become as stagnant and dead as our relationship with God. Our actions will reflect the truth about what is really happening in our heart. This truth is so important that Jesus says it three different ways in John 14:

"If you love me, obey my commandments" (v. 15).

"Those who accept my commandments and obey them are the ones who love me" (v. 21).

"All who love me will do what I say. My Father will love them, and we will come and make our home with each of them. Anyone who doesn't love me will not obey me" (vv. 23–24).

Obedience and love are inseparable. We cannot claim we love God and live in disobedience to His Word.

"Anyone who belongs to God listens gladly to the words of God. But you don't listen because you don't belong to God" (John 8:47).

Black and white: You do not listen because you do not belong to God. There is no self-justification on the planet that can manipulate its way around this truth. Either I love Him—or—I love me. Which does my life support? Is my life pouring out in the pursuit of God through loving obedience—or—is it pouring out in the pursuit of comfort through self-loving justification?

"Love means doing what God has commanded us, and he has commanded us to love one another" (2 John 1:6).

Am I truly loving God by doing what He has asked? Am I loving others in every way He asks me to?

In this heart, authentic obedience is not one thing, but three things. Simply saying yes is not enough. My "yes" needs to be firmly accompanied by my actions. Specifically, I need to do what He asks: 1) immediately, 2) to the best of my ability and 3) with a joyful attitude. Like the teenager who has been asked to clean his or her room, I can say, "Yes" but have no intention of cleaning my room until the next century. I can say, "Yes" and pick up one pair of boots and kick everything else halfway under my bed. I can say, "Yes" and storm into my room and slam the door. None of these responses, or any combination of them, is true obedience or agreement.

When I was a young teen, my grandfather asked me to help him haul compost. We needed to shovel up the aged manure into a wheelbarrow and push it fifty yards and dump it in the garden plot. I agreed and went to fetch another wheelbarrow. Instantly, I knew it had a flat tire. I did not want to take the time to pump it up. And I did not think it mattered that I pumped it up.

So I set out to "help," intentionally choosing not to be prepared. Instantly, I experienced the penalties of my selfish decision by how much heavier and harder it was to push a full wheelbarrow with a flat tire. I was not able to keep up with my grandpa. He, with a full tire, had enough breath to whistle as he worked. I was so tired, all I wanted to do was sit on the poop pile and complain. Without saying a word, he taught me a life lesson that still resonates in my heart to this day.

Time to stop pretending to serve God with a spiritual flat.

Before God, our procrastination, half-heartedness and begrudging attitude contradict anything we claim as loving obedience. Instead, these negative attributes expose what is true—we do not love Him as much as we say.

No father desires a relationship with their child that is hallmarked by these selfish traits. Why? Because the genuine love of the child for their parent will naturally eliminate these things.

"My sheep listen to my voice; I know them, and they follow me" (John 10:27).

Genuine love for Dad produces genuine compliance. Indeed, when it comes to obedience, we *are* free to choose . . . but not free from the consequences of our choice.

If a thirty-year-old skater who does not know the voice of the Holy Spirit chooses to obey Him with an open heart and without question . . . how much more should the redeemed?

"I have loved you even as the Father has loved me. Remain in my love. When you obey my commandments, you remain in my love, just as I obey my Father's commandments and remain in his love. I have told you these things so that you will be filled with my joy. Yes, your joy will overflow! *This is my commandment: Love each other in the same way I have loved you.*"

John 15:9–12, emphasis added

Pure-hearted obedience is the beautiful result of pure-hearted love for God.

Submission is the natural desire, the overflow of a heart that is deeply in love with its Master. One can fall in love with God in the same manner you fall in love with each other . . . by knowing Him. And this knowing happens when you listen to His voice—pursuing Him through the beautiful, long, honest love letter of His Word. By aligning and planting each word to grow into the deep soil of your heart every day—renewed obedience is the luscious fruit of His cultivated love within you.

By seeking Him through His Word every day, you willingly position your heart within His heart. By standing beneath the waterfall of His love, you are daily filled to overflowing. The outpouring of His love to others is the balance of what you are choosing to receive from Him.

This is the beautiful bedrock of revival—the natural outpouring of the Father's love through those who daily, purposefully live within the presence of His love.

Lord Jesus,

I choose to renew my obedience to You, Your Word, Your voice by doing what You ask simply because I love You.

I don't want to be half-hearted anymore. I don't want to give You my spiritual leftovers of, "Maybe I'll get to it. Maybe I'll try. Maybe I'll be joyful." I'm worn out from pretending to serve You with a spiritual flat in my heart.

I'm done sitting on the poop pile of my complacency and control and complaining about how hard it is to serve You.

Today, I commit to pump up my flat heart with the truth of Your Word. I commit to know You by—daily—reading Your beautiful love letter to me and positioning it to grow deep roots within this life.

No more do I simply want to know about Your love—I choose Your love to become the foundation of who I am.

I choose to pursue You.

Right now, my God, I choose to stand every day under the waterfall of Your presence. I lift this vessel to be filled to overflowing with Your love. From this place, when the world bumps into me, You are what sloshes out—Your love all over them.

I acknowledge that my pure-hearted obedience will become the beautiful result of my pure-hearted love for You, my heavenly Dad.

Amen.

NINE

Renew My Belief

*Jesus, please renew my belief that when I'm
standing fully in Your presence, Your powerful
love through me can do anything.*

I pray that . . . you can understand the confident hope he
has given to those he called . . . the incredible greatness
of God's power for us who believe him.

Ephesians 1:18–19

As previously mentioned, I love the wild regions. These
places are where I hear the voice of my God most clearly
and see His truth reflected most vividly. Introduced into my life
in early childhood, Castle Craigs remains among my personal
hall of fame hikes for experiencing the wonder of our God.
Although I have climbed it through every season of my life,
each ascent is filled with the comfort of old memories and the
marvelous awe of making new ones.

In keeping with the Cascade mountain range, Castle Craigs
was birthed through fire and ice. Like its titanic sister to the

north, Mount Shasta, the Craigs were also forged through volcanic origins and shaped by glaciation. The jaw-dropping result is a vast, jumbled range of gray spires. These granite pinnacles range from two hundred feet to over six thousand feet in height. A solitary trail leads the stout of heart up into a saddle cradled between the interlocking arms of these giants. Only one of the monoliths, the Castle Dome, offers the slightest invitation to be explored.

This imposing tower juts nearly five thousand feet into the vast blue of the Northern California sky. From any viewpoint below, this ascension looks too high, too vertical, too impossible. From below, the single occluded trail remains unseen. It threads through a brushy forest that transitions into alpine terrain, then circles up through the spires and around to the back of the beast, where it ends. From this perspective, the summit of the dome is three hundred feet of very steep, smooth granite.

Here, at higher altitudes, hikers can take advantage of a unique feature carved within the stone that looks like rain channels. These grooves form a riveted passage up a good distance of the west side. Although this is not hard to scale, the exposure is real. Any slip where purchase is lost would send a climber sliding into sudden peril. But for the sure-footed and confident of heart, this place leads upward to the dome shoulder. As if you were hiking over the literal shoulder of a giant, this flattish place is easy, safe, protected. But the passage beyond the shoulder leads from easy and protected to the extreme exposure of the eastern face.

The eastern wall is so vertical that the climber perceives it is undercut; there is nothing in front but a vast, windy void. On this side of the dome, the full stance of its elevation is exposed, several thousand feet of straight down. To navigate this face, one must cross what is best described as a bowl tipped to resemble a 45-degree slope. Walking across the bowl feature is in itself not hard, but the result if you lost your footing would be catastrophic.

Once across the bowl, the route leads to a large ledge. Like a grimace on the side of a cliff, it yawns open with enough height to stand in. From this place, there appears to be no exit, no way out—just a trap on a shelf that opens into nothing but thin air. Within this realm, the exposure is so intense, so extreme it engulfs all who enter with the ominous sense that nothing awaits but total obliteration. It feels like an inescapable fracture of fear, a crevasse of cataclysm, a crack of death, the place where one might die.

This is my favorite moment of the climb.

I love this foreboding crack because it takes those who dare to venture into its menacing jaws—straight into the dominion of belief.

If I could see with my eyes this journey of faith before our God, often it would look like this crack—capturing all who enter in the vise grip of fear, the overarching dread that you will never survive what God is calling you to do. From this place, we cry out, *Lord, this is impossible! I cannot survive what You are asking me to do. There is no way out of this place of pain. I cannot step in any direction, for each will lead to my utter destruction. God, where are You in this?*

He is right where He has always been—still on the throne, still in control, still worthy of our praise and still the King for which nothing is impossible.

For my wild heart, what makes this ledge of terror hallowed ground is what He has taught me here. In this place, only when I walk nearly as far as I can go out into the crack, into where every sense screams for me to turn back, can His truth be seen.

Opposite from the yawning expanse of death, in the tower of granite itself, is a narrow crack, a passage through the impossible. The way has always existed but remains unseen—until I stand on the ledge.

Not until focus is broken off the deadly exposure, and refocused on the rock, is the passage discovered.

The entire dome is completely cracked in half. A narrow split runs nearly the rest of the climb to the summit. You cannot fall. Towering stone walls hold you safely from either side. As one exits the crack, a relatively short bit of bouldering leads to one of the most glorious summits within the Pacific Northwest.

The point of the parable is this: Every life will face multiple "cracks of death." Each of us will have seasons where we believe there is no way out of our hardships and another step will lead to our complete destruction. Yet from our Father's perspective, these are the hallowed places that lead us into absolute reliance on Him alone. Every crack of death is worth that.

We were crushed and overwhelmed beyond our ability to endure, and we thought we would never live through it. In fact, we expected to die. But as a result, *we stopped relying on ourselves and learned to rely only on God*, who raises the dead. And he did rescue us from mortal danger, and he will rescue us again. We have *placed our confidence in him, and he will continue to rescue us.*

2 Corinthians 1:8–10, emphasis added

With Jesus, there is always a way through every obstacle of pain we will ever face. And nearly always, that passage will not become clear until we are standing in the very realm of what our every sense proclaims is impossible.

In this exact place our impossible is broken off to make way for His always possible.

This is where our belief in Him *over all other things* is forged. This is where we choose to stop focusing on all that can destroy us—and start focusing on the only One who can save us.

Much of our life in Christ reflects this. Often, we cannot see the way. But we can always see Jesus—and He is "the way, the truth, and the life" (John 14:6). The portions of our journey that appear impossible, the bits that make us feel as if we might die if we try, are the steps that require us to believe less in us—and more in Him.

Because of Him, we "confidently trust the LORD" to take care of us. Because of Him, we "are confident and fearless and can face [our] foes triumphantly" (Psalm 112:7–8).

There is no faithlessness of men on the planet that can overrule the power of the proclamation that "Jesus Christ is the same yesterday, today, and forever" (Hebrews 13:8). Our lack of belief does not change the fact that everything Jesus did when He walked this earth, He is still doing through those who honestly believe that He can.

I have a friend who often says, "Even an underdog under God is unstoppable!" Which are you? Stopped by your unbelief—or unstoppable because of your belief?

When we truly believe something, that belief changes our actions.

Do your actions proclaim that your faith is greater than your fear, pride or complacency? Or do fear, pride and complacency rule your heart? What directs your actions? What does the fruit of your life proclaim?

> What good is it, dear brothers and sisters, if you say you have faith but don't show it by your actions? Can that kind of faith save anyone? Suppose you see a brother or sister who has no food or clothing, and you say, "Good-bye and have a good day; stay warm and eat well"—but then you don't give that person any food or clothing. What good does that do? So you see, *faith by itself isn't enough. Unless it produces good deeds, it is dead and useless.*
>
> James 2:14–17, emphasis added

Unshakable belief in Jesus Christ has the power to transform the world around us. But is it? Is the outpouring of the Spirit of the living God through us impacting and igniting the world around us?

Throughout the gospels Jesus teaches something stunning. The people He taught in the synagogue of his hometown, Nazareth, "were deeply offended and refused to believe in him. Then Jesus told them, 'A prophet is honored everywhere except in his own hometown and among his own family.' And so *he did only a few miracles there because of their unbelief*" (Matthew 13:57–58, emphasis added).

Because of their unbelief, His miraculous power was not released—not because He did not have the power, but because they did not believe in His power. Equally, when those who gathered around Jesus believed Him, His power was released into their every circumstance (see Matthew 9:1–7, 18–34; Mark 5:34; 9:23; 10:52; Luke 7:36–50; 8:26–56; 17:19). Our belief that Jesus can enter our situations, and transform them, becomes the supernatural fuel that ignites His miracles.

Two blind men followed along behind [Jesus]. . . .

They went right into the house where he was staying, and Jesus asked them, "Do you believe I can make you see?"

"Yes, Lord," they told him, "we do."

Then he touched their eyes and said, "*Because of your faith, it will happen.*" Then their eyes were opened, and they could see!

Matthew 9:27–30, emphasis added

Belief becomes breakthrough.

Our belief in God's authority to lead us does not materialize when we are sitting on the couch reading about it. It is established when we hear His voice calling us to walk through a crowd toward the one, a single individual who is suffering in silence. Our belief in God is developed when we trust Him enough to pursue His will out onto the deadly ledge of our pride, past our complacency, beyond our paralyzing fear toward that son, that daughter, the one who needs to hear of His redeeming love.

In this place, where our life is wholly His, genuine belief arises from our deepest gratitude—out of a heart that knows it deserves death, but instead has been given life. And with this gift of His life to us, we give His gift of life to others through the belief, the knowing that we have been saved by His love and we belong to Him forever.

"The LORD is my strength and shield. *I trust him with all my heart.* He helps me, and my heart is filled with joy. I burst out in songs of thanksgiving" (Psalm 28:7, emphasis added).

There is no "crack of death" so great that His love for you is not greater still.

With His unquenchable love, He calls you out onto the ledge where belief is challenged and exercised into faith. And this faith compels you to keep walking, keep trusting Him for every step through your valley of the shadow of death.

This region of destruction will only look scary when your focus is on the scary things. But when we fix our gaze on Him, no ledge, no lions, no legion of enemies, no lull of death will shake our focus from the One who holds us securely, the One who leads us home.

"'But you are my witnesses, O Israel!' says the LORD. 'You are my servant. You have been chosen to know me, believe in me, and understand that I alone am God. There is no other God—there never has been, and there never will be'" (Isaiah 43:10).

Friend, you have been chosen to know God. You have been called out to believe in Him and understand that He is the one and only King, who beckons you to trust in Him more than all other things.

Today, reestablish Him alone as your Lord and stand up in your unshakable belief that there is no terrifying ledge in this world that overshadows His ability to lead you through to the passage that is His love. When our belief is in Him alone, there is always a way. And by faith, we can trust Him for every single step.

How do we move into greater belief? We simply take the next step out onto the ledge of trusting Him more than all other things.

Paul wrote, "I pray that your hearts will be flooded with light so that you can understand the confident hope he has given to those he called—his holy people who are his rich and glorious inheritance" (Ephesians 1:18). He continued, "I also pray that you will understand the incredible greatness of God's power for us who believe him" (v. 19).

Castle Craigs reflects this truth. It is not until your focus is broken off the deadly exposure, and refocused on the Rock, that the way is discovered. The passage through our impossible has always existed; it simply remains unseen until we trust Him enough to walk out and stand on the ledge of pure belief in our God.

For our every crack of death . . . belief becomes breakthrough.

My Savior,

Please show me: Is Your presence within me stopped—or unstoppable?

I don't want to be like those in Your hometown who, because of unbelief, drew closed the veil on seeing Your loving power released within them.

I don't want any unbelief to cripple what You are calling into action through me.

Today, I leap into the truth of Your Word and grasp the full measure of "understanding the incredible greatness of Your power for us who believe in You."

I choose to break off my focus on any deadly exposure and refocus on You—the Rock of my salvation.

I acknowledge that pure belief in You will lead me through every "crack of death" I will ever face.

I believe that You alone will guide my steps out onto the narrow ledge of trust . . . right up to the beautiful passage through the mountain of unbelief.

By believing in You more than all other things, all other things will crack in half, and I will walk right on through into Your glorious presence.

In this stunning place . . . from this day forward . . . is where I choose to live.

Jesus, with all that is within me, I love all that You are, and I trust You for every step to come.

Amen.

TEN

Renew My Joy

Jesus, renew the signature of Your joy in my heart.

"These things I have spoken to you, that My joy may
remain in you, and that your joy may be full."

John 15:11 NKJV

Rain fell in great gray sheets. Drenched sheep scattered off
the dirt road as we bounced onward through a vast array of
mud-filled potholes. Finally, we reached a large metal gate with
a sign proclaiming we had indeed reached our destination—one
of the few therapeutic riding centers just outside the town of
Timisoara, Romania. It was the last day of our trip.

Months earlier, I had been summoned by Beautiful Gate
Ministries, an organization that spreads the Gospel through
impoverished countries by translating women's devotional materials. Judy, my beloved friend, assistant and prayer warrior,
and I were asked to join a small team that would travel through
Eastern Europe and share the hope of Jesus Christ.

For the past thirteen days, we had traveled between two to
five hours a day while speaking one to four times a day. Having

already journeyed through much of Moldova sharing the message of salvation, we were now nearing the finish of doing the same in Romania. The purpose of our next event was to share with professional equine therapists how Crystal Peaks Youth Ranch works with all children, including those with disabilities. Although they were not faith based, I would also be demonstrating how to support kids with the love of Jesus Christ.

Heavy rain forced us to meet upstairs in a simple room. In a country that wastes nothing, the furnishings were lovingly made from discarded wooden pallets. After sharing a simple meal with us, the group pushed their plates aside and launched into a series of kid-related and horse-related questions.

In moments, it was clear that this crowd was highly steeped in "therapy models," human understanding and programming. My encouragements to see each child as an individual and pray over them were instantly crushed between eyebrows crashing together in frustration.

While listening to one leader speak of the value of balance and movement, which is important, my grandmother's favorite Bible verse danced across my mind: "Trust in the LORD with all your heart, and lean not on your own understanding; in all your ways acknowledge *Him*, and *He* shall direct your paths" (Proverbs 3:5–6 NKJV, emphasis added).

Flowing out above our conversation was my simple prayer: *Jesus, when You are not present in a life, when You are not first, the wisdom of men is. The "therapy of men" never saved or healed anyone—ever. It is merely a lonely counterfeit, a Band-Aid of logic that won't stick. Only Your redeeming love heals all that is broken. Lord, please show me how to pour out Your hope and joy in a way that they can see the difference, that they can see You, that they can see Your gift of redemption for them.*

The assembly moved outside and across a muddy yard into a covered arena. Here, I was expected to give a "therapeutic demonstration" of how to work with a disabled child. I watched as a dark-haired boy was led by the hand into the arena. The leader informed me that the "subject" was an autistic thirteen-year-old who was blind from birth. His name was Cristian. Right behind him, a short Haflinger-type gelding was led in with a riding pad strapped to his back. A pair of assistants were assigned to me. One was tasked to lead the horse and the second to walk along the off side of the gelding in case our rider needed help to balance. This individual would also aid in translation when needed.

During my formal introduction with Cristian, I was delighted that he spoke some English. I was also struck by his expression. Although he was being led through a world of darkness, his countenance was one of pure contentment. He was about five feet tall. His black hair and cloudy dark eyes framed such a sweet face. He was a happy little man who seemed comfortable living within an unseeing body. Over the years of working with kids, I have noticed that when one sense is deficit, other senses fill in the missing gaps—often in the most unique and beautiful ways. Cristian's eyes did not work, but his mind was bright and inquisitive.

My heart rose above the institutional learning environment and prayed, *Jesus, You made him perfect. He's Yours. He's Your son. He's so much more than a "subject" to simply stretch, bend and balance. He's a little boy who needs to feel seen and valued. Lord, he needs to feel love; he needs to feel Your love. Lead on, Holy Spirit . . . and I will follow.*

After a brief introduction, I led Cristian over to the horse.

While placing his small hands gently on the gelding's side, I asked, "Cristian, who is this horse?"

Without thought, he answered, "Jax. He's the horse I always ride."

I felt led to inquire again, "Buddy, who is this horse to you?"

Turning slightly toward me, he grinned. "He's my friend."

"Is Jax a casual friend? Or a really good friend?"

Cristian's smile grew. "He's a really good friend!"

"Wow! That's great! I bet you know he's a really good friend because he gives you really good gifts, like riding on his back!"

With a toothy grin, Cristian nodded.

"Well, if Jax gives you good gifts . . . what can you give him back? What would be a good gift given back to him?"

My young friend pondered this question for a long moment.

Finally, I gave him a suggestion. "I think he would really like it if you would 'tell him with your touch' that you love him and he's your good friend. Do you think that's a good idea?"

Again, he smiled and gave a hearty nod.

Guiding him with my hands, together we rubbed Jax's muzzle, eyes, ears, chest, shoulders and rump. With our good gift firmly in place, it was finally time to climb aboard the gelding's back. Nearly in stride, our little group set off around the arena, still under the heavy scrutiny of those watching.

I had a silly flashback of feeling the pressure of showing livestock when I was a kid in 4-H. I was highly aware of the therapists and equally aware that none of what I was doing fit within the parameters of the equine therapy they were familiar with.

Yet to respect their profession and the education they lived by, I encouraged Cristian to show his love for his horse by reaching as far as he could with his hands and feet to rub Jax all the way from ears to rump. I even had Cristian ride his horse backward and facing each side, while the horse was walking, so he could reach and show love to even more of his equine buddy. By doing this, my young friend was challenged to maintain his balance in a variety of awkward positions, thus satisfying a portion of conventional therapy.

But there is nothing conventional about Jesus Christ and how He moves within the hearts of men. He defies our laws of reason and supersedes any boundary assigned by our human understanding. His love is wild, and He colors outside the lines of our comprehension. Once we experience His overwhelming hope and joy, nothing else in the realm of men can compare.

Jesus, as this beautiful boy is pouring out his gift of love over his horse, will You pour out Your gift of love over him? Do this, Lord, in a way that his unique mind will understand how treasured he is to You and to this world . . . exactly how he is.

"Cristian, now that you've loved your horse well and given him a really good gift, I think he would like to give you another gift in return. I think he would like you to trot with him. Trotting is a little bit faster than walking, and it's a lot more bumpy. Does that sound scary or fun?"

With little hesitation, he replied, "Fun! Trotting sounds like fun!"

With a few simple instructions in place, our crew encouraged horse and boy into a more challenging gait. Unexpectedly, Jax burst into a lively trot. Cristian's upper body lurched backward with the new momentum. In sudden response, he let out a voice-cracking cry that alternated between half man and half child.

Was this a sound of fear . . . or elation?

I whipped around to look at his face.

That is when I saw a rift between heaven and earth open. Pure joy was streaming out through this boy's huge smile.

I nearly fell to my knees as the group trotted past. I yelled from behind them, "Cristian! Your smile! It's amazing! I've never seen anything so beautiful! Don't stop ever!"

He did not.

Lap after delightful trotting lap, what I thought was glorious only grew bigger and brighter with every stride. I could literally feel the loving presence of Jesus pouring over and through him. His laughter was filling the arena. The very presence of God's joy was beaming through a boy—a boy the world considers a blind and broken "subject."

After a few full victory laps around the arena, the little team pulled up and stopped in front of the panel of professionals and me.

Out of breath, Cristian looked in the direction where he thought I was standing and shouted, "I have a beautiful smile! Can you see it? Mrs. Kim, can you *see it*?"

I saw it. The panel saw it—and every angel in heaven saw it. We all witnessed Cristian transform within the presence of pure joy.

He was seen. He was valued. He was flooded with the love of God. In response, his whole body was laughing.

The therapy team was stunned. They only knew Cristian as a quiet boy . . . right up until the moment white-hot joy burned through his darkness and ignited his heart with holy gladness.

I was still gushing about the beauty and power of his smile when he stopped me with a simple question. "Tell me . . . Mrs. Kim . . . what does my smile look like?"

My prayer was nothing more than, *Speak, Jesus.*

I approached boy and horse. Reaching for where his hands tightly gripped Jax's mane, I placed both of my hands over his. Looking up into his unfocused eyes, I leaned in, "Cristian, imagine when it's early in the morning. You're awake and it's dark and cold. Then the sun breaks over the horizon and streams into your room. You know the sun has risen because you can *feel* its heat on your skin. Suddenly, everything around you is drenched in light and warmth."

I continued, "Your smile is like that! It fills and warms the whole room, this whole arena . . . and everyone in it! Cristian, your smile is so beautiful that it encourages *me* to smile. Through your smile, your joy becomes my joy. Please don't ever stop smiling. It's such a good gift! Your smile has blessed me more than words can say. Thank you for that, for sharing your glorious smile with me. Now I have a smile, too."

His childlike expression changed. The wheels of human understanding were turning. Flesh was encountering and receiving Spirit. Truth, love, joy were rooting in fertile soil. Cristian was comprehending the power of the gift he was given—and the gift he could give.

With my hands still cupped over his, he leaned toward me and asked quietly, "Mrs. Kim, what does your smile look like?"

I could not restrain the tears filling my eyes. "My smile is different than yours. Why don't you tell me what *you* think it looks like?" With that simple instruction, I gently placed his right hand on my face.

With thoughtful wonder, he felt every contour of my smiling cheeks and mouth. To gain the full picture, he even ran his horse-grubby fingers inside my lips. Then, after careful deliberation, he leaned down from Jax's broad back to be closer to me. With his innocent lips only inches from my ear, he whispered, "Your smile is like . . . like . . . the best dream ever!"

From the mouth of a young man who cannot see, one whom the world considers blind and broken, was delivered a precious gift—one of the best gifts ever.

Cristian and I talked a little longer about the power of good gifts. We talked about how Jesus gave the very best gift when He gave His life for us—so we could live for Him. We spoke about how every good gift ultimately comes from Jesus and is meant to live in our hearts. We shared how easy it is for us to give back good gifts to Jesus by choosing to have a grateful heart—a joyful heart that constantly lifts praise and gratitude to Him.

All too soon our time together came to a close. In keeping with the endearing Romanian culture, Cristian and I kissed each other's cheeks many times.

In parting, he gave me one last gift. "Mrs. Kim, from now on when you see the sunrise, no matter where you are, you will remember me and my beautiful smile."

Cristian was right. Indeed, I have.

A demonstration happened all right: Jesus poured out His love for all to witness and experience. Everyone present watched a quiet, blind, autistic boy transform in minutes as the pure molten joy of our Lord healed his heart and revealed a small portion of his value in this world.

The point of the encounter is this: The "fruit of me" cannot heal anyone spiritually. But the fruit of the Spirit, when released through me, can heal all who reach for it.

Genuine joy is the hallmark of the redeemed.

"But the Holy Spirit produces this kind of fruit in our lives: love, *joy*, peace, patience, kindness, goodness, faithfulness, gentleness, and self-control. There is no law against these things!" (Galatians 5:22–23, emphasis added).

Among the Holy Spirit's fruit, joy is second only to His love. God's love is all-powerful, and joy is the strong shoulder that carries it into action. If our Lord's love is a river, then His joy is the geyser that showers His living water over everyone present. Pure joy carries the love of God into the environments around us, contacting all with His life. When we release the joy of our God, our God releases even more than His joy over us.

"Don't be dejected and sad, for the joy of the LORD is your strength!" (Nehemiah 8:10).

The beautiful, powerful fruit of joy, within us, becomes strength. Joy produces strength to keep moving forward through our challenges. And this is not all that joy produces within those who choose it: "I pray that God, the source of hope, will *fill you completely with joy* and peace because you trust in him. *Then you will overflow with confident hope* through the power of the Holy Spirit" (Romans 15:13, emphasis added).

When we choose joy within our challenges, God promises to give us strength *and* hope. We are literally designed to overflow with the crazy-amazing abundance of His joy. The pure molten joy of Jesus Christ cannot be shackled, imprisoned or contained by anything in this world. Like a holy river flowing from the heart of God, it breaks through every bond and boundary we will ever know.

"Let all who take refuge in you rejoice; let them sing joyful praises forever. Spread your protection over them, that all who love your name may be filled with joy" (Psalm 5:11).

Joy is among the strongest of our hallowed arrows. These holy weapons are gifted to those who receive the Holy Spirit— and our enemy has no defense against them. Wherever we intentionally release the arsenal of His joy, hope, strength and freedom, darkness is overwhelmed by the glory of our King's brilliant wake.

This is the joy of our God.

"The Word gave life to everything that was created, and his life brought light to everyone. The light shines in the darkness, and the darkness can never extinguish it" (John 1:4–5).

Handling the joy of our Jesus is like handling spiritual honey. It was always our heavenly Dad's desire that the more we handle His joy, the more we are covered by its golden goodness from head to toe.

Releasing His joy means wearing it yourself.

Friend, if you still have breath, you still have opportunity for giving a good gift, the gift of our Father's joy. God's Word encourages us to "make the most of every opportunity" for doing good; to be "filled with the Holy Spirit"; and to "give thanks for everything to God the Father in the name of our Lord Jesus Christ" (Ephesians 5:16, 18, 20).

So on this day, be encouraged to ask Jesus what good gift *you* might give to another who needs to know His joy. Ask Him where you can release the living "spiritual honey" of His glad presence.

Jesus said, "I have told you these things so that you will be filled with my joy. Yes, your joy will overflow!" (John 15:11).

Peter wrote, "You love him even though you have never seen him. Though you do not see him now, you trust him; and you rejoice with a glorious, inexpressible joy" (1 Peter 1:8).

When we know, really know, who we are in Christ, the undeniable result is the "fire hose effect"—His joy filling us and pouring through us, bringing life to all those we release it over.

So how do you *really* know who you are in Christ? The same way you really know anyone: You spend as much time with that person as possible. You ask questions; you devour his or her every word.

"When I discovered your words, I devoured them. They are my joy and my heart's delight, for I bear your name, O LORD God of Heaven's Armies" (Jeremiah 15:16).

The revival of His joy begins within your heart when you discover God's Word—and devour it.

Indeed, genuine joy is the hallmark of the redeemed.

This is where we gain His strength. This is where we are filled with His hope. This is the overflow of His joy.

Beloved Savior,

No one can steal my joy, not even Satan himself, unless I choose to give it to him.

Your rampant joy is second only to the almighty power of Your love.

You freely offer me joy as one of the deadliest weapons of warfare against my foes of fear, angst, oppression and depression.

The strong arrows of Your joy, fired again and again, destroy them all.

The truth of Your Word, bite for delicious bite, fills me with Your joy. And right now, I commit to devour it every day.

By filling myself with Your joy, the overflow of that joy will transform the world around me.

Releasing Your joy makes me stronger.

Releasing Your joy makes me even more hopeful.

Releasing Your joy covers me with the golden goodness of this spiritual honey.

Today, I choose to relinquish my focus on what is not— for what is.

You love me, I am chosen by You. I am Your child. I am enfolded within Your love forever.

Knowing this truth ignites my heart in the flame of joy.

You have me; I have You. That is enough to live consumed in Your joy for the rest of my days.

Jesus, today I commit to the renewal of Your joy in me by daily filling my heart with Your Word.

So daily I can be poured out.

So daily this life will reflect Your genuine joy as the hallmark of the redeemed.

With my life, Jesus, I love You.

Amen.

ELEVEN

Renew My Purity

Father God, it is the pure of heart who will see Your face. Today, I pursue the renewal of purifying my heart so that no veil of sin will separate our eyes.

Come close to God, and God will come close to you. Wash your hands, you sinners; purify your hearts, for your loyalty is divided between God and the world.

James 4:8

It was midsummer. To celebrate my friend Judy's sixtieth birthday, and nearly a decade of working in ministry side by side, I ambushed her with a surprise trip to fish the wild waters of Alaska.

Sitka was my choice.

This beautiful fishing village balances on a sliver of land compressed between a jagged snow-covered skyline and the vast Gulf of Alaska. The tiny hamlet is located on Baranof Island, which is puzzle-pieced amongst a stunning archipelago of more than two thousand four hundred islands. With only fourteen miles of road system at their disposal, most of the cars of Sitka's residents . . . are boats. Cast within this glorious backdrop, travel in any direction is an adventure.

Part of the surprise for my dear friend was four days of guided fishing. Our time on the sea would be split between angling beyond the capes in the expansive Alaskan Gulf and, when stormy weather blew in, we would duck into the protection of the barrier islands.

Our guide's name was Dan. He was young, energetic and instantly likeable. Accompanied by his enthusiasm for his trade, he was encouraging, selfless and quick to laugh. A native-born Alaskan, he navigated the dizzyingly complex network of channels with the same easy confidence by which his blood traveled within his veins.

After considering the weather and tide constraints, we planned to fish in the open water early before wind and waves made it unsafe. In the deep waters, we would try to limit on king salmon first, halibut second, and then as the heavy water came in, we would find shelter among the islands and finish our day by angling for rockfish. For this wild girl's heart, it sounded like a perfect plan.

At 5:45 a.m. the following day, Judy and I followed Dan down the dock and boarded his boat. It was already raining, and even the protective water amid the islands was tossed into steep waves. On this day, traveling beyond the cape would be ill-advised for our thirty-foot boat, so we trolled for salmon behind an island with nearly vertical green walls. Even from under the low gray sky, great fingers of glacial ice could be seen cupping the mountains in a timeless frozen embrace.

Standing on the deck of our wave-tossed boat, my heart soaring in the presence of the One who made it all, I was home in the church of His presence. Fishing faded before the physical power of this land. The reflection of His glory was overwhelming. With my hands over my heart, I soaked in the wonder of His awe-inspiring beauty.

This I know: Life does not have to be perfect . . . to still be wonderful.

Hours flew by like hallowed minutes. My heart rose through a canvas cast within the deepest shades of green and blue—we were still fishing. With no bites behind the protection of the island, Dan made the decision to move toward another one of his fishing hot spots. But to get there, we would need to cross the main channel through which the wind and waves were now funneling.

To avoid seasickness, Judy sat completely vertical in the co-pilot's seat as Dan turned the boat out into the channel. With nothing to challenge their power in this wind-swept place, the waves grew larger and larger. Soon, when we slid into the well of the waves, they reached higher than the boat itself.

Our vessel felt more like a cork bobbing between the peaks and valleys of the growing seas. Repeatedly, the boat would rise high on the crest of a wave, only to have the wind blow its opposing face into a concave surface that was not capable of sustaining the weight. The boat would balance momentarily on the peak and then fall as if being dropped from the sky. Every fall from the top of a wave ended with the same violent, knee-buckling, disc-crushing, molar-shattering crunch.

Twice my dear friend looked at me with raised eyebrows, wordlessly asking, *Are we going to die? Is this okay?* Twice I nodded toward Dan, whose conversation never missed a beat, silently answering, *All is well.*

When the channel was finally behind us, the open sea softened into substantial rollers. Even though the waves were still huge, without the sharp peaks, it was easier to stand and continue fishing. In no time, we retrieved the salmon gear and began fishing again.

Since Judy was the birthday girl, it was determined that she would reel in the first salmon. After a few missed bites, she gained a feel for the rod, and the next hit she hooked quickly.

Weight and behavior gave witness that the salmon was large and aggressive. While Judy reeled as fast as she could, the salmon led her up the port side, across the bow, and down the starboard side. She chased the fish in a twenty-minute rodeo lap before finally netting it. Her first king salmon of the trip came over the rail at well over half her height. The picture of her laughing while trying to bear-hug it like a giant bar of soap will remain as one of my favorite memories of the adventure.

By the next day, the weather had swung like a celestial pendulum from tumultuous to equally placid. Joined by a delightful father-and-son team, we streamed across an ocean surface so glassy that it looked more like liquid oil than water. Together, we glided out past the cape and into the gulf. In no time, the salmon box was filled, so we powered up the main engines and motored farther out into the indescribable blue of deeper water to hunt for halibut.

As an avid fisherman and first mate on our own guide boat in Oregon, I am always intrigued by each unique fishery and the rigging needed for success. After we stowed away the long, graceful salmon rods in favor of short, stocky halibut rods, Dan retrieved circle hooks so large that they were nearly the size of my crooked finger. Two hooks were affixed on each line and then loaded with a smorgasbord of greasy bait. A two-pound weight was added to ensure that the sordid buffet reached the ocean floor. Once compiled, the whole ensemble was lowered into the depths.

Alaskan regulations require that when halibut fishing with a guide, the legal size to keep is 36 inches and below, or 80 inches and above. If we chose to fish without a guide, all sizes are legal. Once the gear was on the sea floor, we were prepared for what could be a very long wait. But as our God continued to bless, in minutes the tip of the stiff rod started to bob. This was the telling indication that far below, a large bottom fish was sampling the greasy fare.

Instantly, Judy started to reel up on the fish . . . and reel and reel and reel—all 380 feet of line. What rose from the deep was the largest rockfish I had ever seen. Because it was a protected species, we carefully released it to return to the ocean floor. After applying fresh bait, we sent the gear back into the depths. Again, in only minutes, she had another taker. With arms still burning from the last retrieval, she set about hauling up the next fish.

This was a much heavier fish.

I watched my dear friend recruit every muscle she had to coax this beast up to the surface. Slowly, the bait taker rose into view—a thirty-inch halibut. Cheering together, we jumped up and down like two six-year-olds, thanking Jesus for the delicious provision.

Our time out in the deep continued to provide bountifully. More halibut came over the rail, along with lingcod and rockfish. All the while, the sea, smiling in glistening agreement, became more and more glassy.

Finally, it was time to head into shallower waters and fill our tags with tasty black rockfish. Dan guided his boat into a beautiful small bay with water so cobalt clear that you could nearly see the bottom thirty feet below. Again, we swapped the stubby hundred-pound lined halibut rods for smaller rods with lighter lines to catch smaller, lighter fish. In comparison, the gear felt like a toy, a plastic pink Barbie rod you would give to a small child. The fish we were hunting are pelagic, usually living in the water column above rocky points. So this species required that we drop our bait to about twenty feet and reel through their ranks.

My first pass made me laugh out loud. A dozen black rockfish chased the bait to the surface in an aggressive, ravenous feeding frenzy. I was so fascinated by their strong, predatory behavior that catching them fell secondary to simply watching them attack whatever passed through their midst.

During this time, the son of the father-son duo caught a large lingcod. Being a voracious predator, it had a wide pre-historic mouth filled with menacing daggers. Its beige skin was dappled with the most detailed and intricate pattern of brown and copper spots I had ever encountered. Somehow, it was the most beautiful-yet-ugly fish I had ever seen. Intrigued, I wanted to try to catch one.

Because lingcod are a true bottom fish, I would need to send my bait down to the sea floor and jig it up and down. Dan had just warned our party not to allow our gear to spend too much time on the bottom because it would get hung up in the rocks.

The words had barely left his lips when I felt my hook catch immovable stone. Being a first mate, I knew this would mean the entire boat stopping, everyone reeling up and having to wait while the boat backed up to free the gear he just asked us not to stick. Why? Because the silly woman in the back of the boat was not listening.

I did not want to be that careless client who interrupted everyone's day. So, out of embarrassment and pride, I decided to try to dislodge the gear without being noticed. I silently reasoned: *I've freed a zillion rods in Oregon coastal waters. How hard can Alaskan waters be?*

Casually, I reeled down to take as much slack out of the monofilament as I could. I would need strong tension, in the opposite direction, to loosen the hook. Once the slack was out, I thumbed the spool and pulled multiple times from several different directions.

No matter what I tried, I could not seem to find the right angle to free the hook. As the boat drifted away from where my gear was jammed, the 25-pound line was stretching and my rod was bending so hard that the tip was now underwater. Without release, it would break off in moments.

Giving one final heave, I felt the gear move. It was coming up. Heartened, I lifted hard again.

Then, I felt something unexpected. The stone pulled back! What I had perceived as "rocks" in which my gear had been wedged was now actively swimming away.

This fish was so heavy it spooled out my line like thread. Because it was now swimming away from the direction of our drift, I laughed and said to our captain, "Umm . . . I think I have a really *big* fish!"

Dan and the rest of the crew turned to see the light rockfish rod bent into the sea like a twig. In a single step, Dan was at the rear controls of the boat and was carefully backing up in the direction of my line.

Through a fishing rod, I had never lifted anything so heavy in my life. It felt like trying to reel up a tractor tire. Except the tire kept redirecting—moving wherever it wished.

The excitement on the boat was rising.

Whatever "this" was, I wanted to see it. I knew the beast that had taken my bait was far larger and more powerful than any of my gear was designed to hold. So my goal was to keep this leviathan on the line through gentle, consistent tension while attempting to turn its head to face the boat.

I could feel my catch turn slowly, then rotate away and spool out reams of line in a lazy plunge back toward the bottom.

Again, I would carefully work to lift its head and turn it toward me.

And yet again, it would rise for a few feet, then meander away in any direction it chose.

Still at the controls, Dan laughed while the rest of the crew gathered around to catch a glimpse of what could be so powerful.

Minutes ticked by. We were still hovering in about thirty feet of water when I was able to coax the monster off the bottom and up into the water column. It rested at twenty feet, seemly unaware it was still hooked. Moving in idle patterns in pure defiance of the steady draw, it swam where it desired. And the tiny thread holding it followed.

Inch by inch, the creature yielded.

Inch by inch, I reeled in line with caution.

The line counter on my reel read eighteen feet, then fifteen feet. Fully one-third of the slender rod was now under water. Minutes were now feeling like days as a steady burn spread up my forearms and into my biceps.

We were at a standoff. An impasse held together by the fragile, equivalent tension of a sliver tied by a thread to a twig.

If I added more pressure, the line would break. I had to casually convince the beast to come my way.

Deadlock.

Time drifted away.

I could not make this fish come to me. At any moment, it could easily snap the line and swim back to freedom. If I were ever to reel it in, I would need to outsmart it in its own environment. I would need it to believe, at all times, it was still in control.

The raging fire in my arms was overwhelmed by my focus on the stalk. I was set on one thing only—catching this fish.

Each moment I felt the fish relax, I would reel in a few more inches. In each new position, I held fast on the pressure. I did not pull or jerk or make any aggressive move. I simply held the tension. As I did, I could literally feel the fish turn its head lethargically to find the position of least resistance, which was always toward me, and I would reel in a bit more line.

No one on board spoke. No one seemed to even breathe as they stood in a circle around me. All eyes were riveted, straining to see something, a shape, a shadow, a movement beneath the sapphire waters.

Inch by inch, fifteen feet was reduced to ten feet. Half my rod was now bent deeply into the sea. As gargantuan as this fish was, I handled it as if I were leading a fawn from cover into clearing. The slightest excess movement would send it dashing away. It had to believe it was still completely in control.

Suddenly, the powerful tension softened.

Matching the release, I reeled up hard and fast.

A mound of water pushed up from below and broke the surface of the sea. A large dark form appeared. Dan recognized it first. "No way! That's a halibut!" he shouted. "A *giant* halibut!"

My mind bent to understand. Halibut are deep-water fish, and we were yards from the shore. I stared at the mottled brown form that had risen to within inches of the boat. It looked more like an old barn door than a fish.

Dan laughed. "That thing's a *monster*! It's nearly as long as you are tall! It's gotta be pushing one hundred fifty pounds!" Then he looked straight at my face with all the seriousness he could muster in the moment. "That . . . should *not* have worked. But it did!" He pointed at the straining gear. "A light rod with 25-pound line . . . *no way* should that have worked! Nice job!"

As much as the gear strained to hold the colossal halibut, my mind strained to hold and comprehend the magnitude of what had just happened.

In quick concession, Dan added, "Because you're being guided today, this halibut is far too big to keep. But if *you* would've been driving this boat, a single gaff hook strike would've landed this beast on your table for the next six months!"

I was astounded.

Dan was right. This halibut was not where it was supposed to be. What should not have worked . . . did. The behemoth fish was lolling in the current right next to the boat—held only by the equivalent of a sliver, attached to a thread, tied to a twig. Yet here it was, caught. And a single, strategic strike would end its life.

As if waking up from an illusion, the goliath fish seemed to suddenly realize it was in mortal danger—after we could have killed it. With a toss of its massive head, it snapped off the steel hook like a pine needle and returned to the depths from which it came.

Although not in the natural, a single strategic strike did land. In the spirit realm, the impact on my own heart was just as powerful. I was stunned by the parable.

Satan's "good enough" is the destroyer of God's best.

"For the LORD sees clearly what a man does, examining every path he takes. An evil man is held captive by his own sins; they are ropes that catch and hold him. He will die for lack of self-control; he will be lost because of his great foolishness" (Proverbs 5:21–23).

How easy it is for a heart to justify "little sin" by comparing it to the world's bigger sin. The truth is, it is still sin, and no matter how small, it still separates us from God. And if that is not deterrent enough, sin of any size leads to our spiritual death (see Romans 6:23).

A fish weighing approximately one hundred fifty pounds was caught on 25-pound line with a tiny hook. It should not have worked. But it did work. It was caught. And had I been self-guided, that fish would be in my freezer.

Sin, all sin, is just like that. What appears as a harmless sliver, connected to a thread and tied to a twig, still has the power to kill.

In God's eyes, there is no such thing as a "small sin," and there should not be in our eyes either.

Our enemy is patient. It is his whisper that fuels the selfish justification that our sin is "no big deal," that it does not control us, it does not hurt anyone, or no one sees. This is exactly what his constant draw sounds like. When we go to "that movie," or watch "that TV series," or hang out in "that place," or engage in "that activity," or partake of "that substance," or view "that website," or speak that slanderous gossip, or forgo time in the Word every morning because "that other thing" is more important than God, this is what the enemy's focus on the stalk looks like.

And when we justify it all by saying something idiotic like, "Well, at least it's not as bad as what *they* are doing," we are turning our head to find that position of least resistance, as we are being reeled inch by inch—away from our God and toward the destruction of our soul.

In times like this, it is Satan who is laughing. It is the enemy of our soul who is slapping the backs of his demonic host and saying, "No way should that have worked! But it did! Nice job!"

Friend, nowhere in God's Word are we prompted to move as close to the world as we can and compare our actions to others to justify our sin. We are called to move away from sin, literally run away from anything that separates us from God and to "pursue righteous living, faithfulness, love, and peace" and "enjoy the companionship of those who call on the Lord with *pure hearts*" (2 Timothy 2:22, emphasis added).

Again, our choice to turn away from our heavenly Dad and pursue sin separates us from His presence. In Isaiah, we see God rejecting His own people for one single reason—idolatry. Idolatry is the delicious bait of choosing to obey other things *more* than God, of making "alliances with pagans" (Isaiah 2:6).

Friend, we cannot make secret alliances with any darkness of this world. We cannot make friends with sin. Any sin. Instead, we must refute the ridiculous justification that since our depravity takes place in private, somehow this makes it okay. The halibut took the bait in private, and it was led to what should have been its last day. Read what Ezekiel said about "hidden sin" in chapter 8 and how much God despises it.

What seems little and insignificant, something that does not control us, something that is "not that bad," is still bad in God's sight.

"Wash yourselves and be clean! Get your sins out of my sight. Give up your evil ways" (Isaiah 1:16).

We cannot encounter revival within our hearts when we are actively pursuing or allowing sin to fill that same heart. Light and darkness cannot share the same place within us. "God is light, and there is no darkness in him at all" (1 John 1:5).

In Ephesians 5:1, we are commanded to imitate Jesus in all things. If there is *no* darkness in Him, we should strive to have none in us.

If Jesus Christ is your Lord and Savior, you carry the Holy Spirit . . . and His first name is "Holy." His holiness will not share space inside us with our continual desire for anything contrary to His presence.

> So put to death the sinful, earthy things lurking within you. Have nothing to do with sexual immorality, impurity, lust, and evil desires. Don't be greedy, for a greedy person is an idolater, worshiping the things of this world. Because of these sins, the anger of God is coming. You used to do these things when your life was still part of this world. But now is the time to get rid of anger, rage, malicious behavior, slander, and dirty language. Don't lie to each other, for you have *stripped off your old sinful nature and all its wicked deeds. Put on your new nature*, and *be renewed* as you learn to *know your Creator and become like him.*
>
> Colossians 3:5–10, emphasis added

Become like Him.

When our desire to become like Him is greater than our desire for all other things, *this* is where purity is renewed. And where purity is thriving, so is the presence of God Himself.

"God blesses those whose hearts are pure, for *they will see God*" (Matthew 5:8, emphasis added).

Hebrews 12:1 encourages us to strip off the sin that "entangles" (AMP, NASB, NIV) or "ensnares" us (NKJV). This is a choice of action. Stripping off sin involves more than simply knowing about sin. It is something we do; we must remove it actively, even aggressively.

Beloved, it is time to *release the bait*; it is time to release the sin, all sin. Because we cannot "run with endurance the race God has set before us" (Hebrews 12:1) *and* run toward junk at the same time. We can only travel in one direction—that which is most important to us.

"When Christ appears . . . we will be like him, for we will see him as he really is. And all who have this eager expectation will *keep themselves pure, just as he is pure*" (1 John 3:2–3, emphasis added). And, "the LORD detests the way of the wicked, but *he loves those who pursue godliness*" (Proverbs 15:9, emphasis added).

Pursuing purity is so precious to our Father's heart that it draws His face, His love and His presence. And *this* is where revival rises.

Lord Jesus,

Wow, wow, wow! When it comes to sin, a sliver, attached to a thread, tied to a twig is the seemingly harmless combination that will draw me away from You . . . toward my death.

I acknowledge that all *sin leads me away from You.*

I've been such a fool. I've allowed "tiny sin" to enter into the heart You gave Your life to redeem.

I've turned my head to find the position of least resistance—instead of turning to You.

The glorious light of Your presence and the deep blackness of my sin cannot fill the same place within me.

I must choose.

Right now I release the bait—I release my sin—and I choose You.

I'm letting go of the enticing lures of this world.

I'm kicking off the sin that has entangled me by naming each one and bringing them to You.

I'm letting go of foolishly believing I was in control of my trajectory. I am not in control. Rather, the life of one who truly believes in You willingly submits to Your control and leadership.

Today, I willingly submit to Your holiness.

I commit to pursue swimming in the freedom of holiness—because You are holy.

I ask, Father, that You wash my mind, purify my heart . . . so when the time is right, I might see Your face.

Thank You for Your patience. Thank You for Your love. Thank You for Your kindness in making a way to purity in Your presence.

I love You forever.

Amen.

REINFORCE MY STRENGTH

Jesus replied, "The most important commandment is this: 'Listen, O Israel! The Lord our God is the one and only Lord. And you must love the Lord your God with all your heart, all your soul, all your mind, and all your *strength*.'"

Mark 12:29–30, emphasis added

TWELVE

Reinforce My Courage

> *Jesus, because You did not back down from*
> *the cross to give me life, I will not back down*
> *from life to give the world Your cross.*

The LORD is my light and my salvation—so why should I be afraid? The LORD is my fortress, protecting me from danger, so why should I tremble? When evil people come to devour me, when my enemies and foes attack me, they will stumble and fall. Though a mighty army surrounds me, *my heart will not be afraid. Even if I am attacked, I will remain confident.*

Psalm 27:1–3, emphasis added

Many years ago, I signed up to serve Native American people through a mission organization in Western Canada. Once our initial training was complete, I was paired with another young woman named Beth. Together, we were assigned to a rural reserve in British Columbia.

The stunning beauty of the surroundings stood in sharp contrast to the terrible pall that hung over the land. We encountered a heavy shroud of oppression, depression and substance abuse the moment our car turned onto this sacred ground. The reserve was located on a sweeping slope of green that was nearly crushed between soaring mountains above and a vast lake below. While cautiously bumping down a lane that was more potholes than road, I had time to consider each dwelling. The poverty was devastating. In a land where winter temperatures reach well below zero, my heart sank to see many homes with no glass in the windows. Abandoned vehicles, trash and dogs mingled together in a silent witness of hopelessness.

Our teeth-shattering ride ended when the road drifted off into impassability. Our "home" for the summer rested close to the shore of a mighty lake. It was a tiny shack that had a door and two windows. There was no power and no water. A long-forgotten outhouse lay down an extremely overgrown trail. When I stepped out of the car, I was greeted by cool wind that moved from the lake surface and stirred beautiful patterns in the tall grass around me.

Beth and I were informed that the shack had been used intermittently for years as a party house. Before we could move in, we would need to shovel up and remove the six inches of broken glass that covered the floor. Supplied with a rake, buckets, a dust pan and broom, we set about making the dilapidated four walls into a home. Two days later the floor was clean, our sleeping mats were laid on the newly scrubbed boards, a few shelves were up in the "kitchen" and we were good to go.

To finish the house, we needed to repair the two glassless window openings. One void was very large, maybe five by six feet, and right next to the front door. When we first arrived, we saw the buildup of broken glass was holding the door closed. It was apparent that the "hole in the wall" next to the door was being used as the entry because it was low enough to easily step through. Our simple solution was to tape layers of plastic grocery bags together and staple them over the opening, allowing light in and keeping cold night air out. Perfect.

The old outhouse made me laugh. Everyone expects a moon cutout in the door. But cutout windows so you could see outside—while seated—was too funny. Whoever built it must have had a peculiar sense of humor, because they also put the latch on the outside of the rickety door. As we got to know and play with the reserve kids, they took delight in hiding within the tall grass in ambush. If we did not see them before entering the outhouse, they would lock us inside for no other reason than to supply pure squealing comedy at watching us try to escape. Seeing those beautiful brown-faced children through the cutouts literally rolling in the grass in the throes of giggle fits remains one of my dearest memories from that powerful season.

Our mission was simple. We were to meet each family on the reserve and simply offer our help in whatever they needed. Our hope was to integrate into their lives through loving service. By helping them gather wood, hunt, garden, build, repair, by cleaning, bringing meals or playing with their kids, we loved them tangibly in an indigenous way—the way they needed most.

Yet for all I gave, I was the one who received the greater blessing. Coexisting with their crushing poverty was an unimaginable wealth. They were a people with a rich culture, marked by a quiet kindness. They were thoughtful and generous. If one family harvested a deer, the entire reserve feasted for a night. *Mine* was a rare word in their realm, and community was not a catchy "Church" word in need of resuscitation. Rather, their community, built on loving respect for others, was the true means by which they had survived for generations. They were fiercely loyal; once their trust was earned, no truer friend existed.

Yet seething within this beautiful indigenous nation was a monster. Moving like a black serpent through each family, it watched, stalking every heart, waiting for the right time to launch an attack. The demonic beast struck with lethal ferocity. Some fought wholeheartedly and were winning. Some fought half-heartedly and were losing. Some stopped fighting . . . and died. The serpent was alcoholism.

Not a family on the reserve was unscathed by its ravages. Alcoholism stole from them all through driving accidents, drowning accidents and rampant suicide. In this tight-knit community, every loss was devastating. With each death, the coils of despair tightened around the hearts of the living. And because hope was missing, we were strategically placed to carry in the presence of hope Himself, Jesus Christ.

As was the way of many, when the work was finished, the fellowship began. This time of togetherness often lasted deep into the night and into the single-digit hours of the morning. Beth and I had been pressing into the heart of a young single mom named Kaila. She had invited us to come to her meager home for dinner. Once the baby was tucked in, we played games. We talked, laughed and listened—for hours. Brick by trusting brick, a friendship was being built. Occasionally, the iron door that guarded her heart would crack open. She would ask bedrock questions such as how we navigated pain, fear or guilt. We were careful to answer in the same manner that we would treat a fearful horse, giving the smallest, clearest answer and then backing up and watching for her next need. We did not crash into her heart, nor did we run away from it. We gave her exactly what she sought in that moment.

As the weeks flew by, the late-night games waned and the soul-searching questions waxed. Kaila's trust was growing stride for stride with her desire to know the God who had saved us, healed us and filled us with His presence. Like a timid flower, her beautiful heart was slowly opening before God's love. No amount of late nights and bleary-eyed mornings stopped us from delivering the Father's redeeming love to His daughter.

Many of our precious evenings ran over into the early hours of the morning. On one such occasion, Beth and I hugged Kaila good night at about 2:00 a.m. and started down the mile-long slope through the reserve that led to our shack. The darkness was no match against the pure glory of the brilliant tapestry overhead. A zillion dazzling stars danced in celestial adoration of the One who created them. Our exhausted hearts could not remain silent in the display. We joined in creation's perpetual worship by lifting our hands, twirling and singing our way down the hill.

Then, about a half mile from our tiny home, we heard a voice . . . a human voice.

Our worship was interrupted by a man shouting out to us. We recognized his tone; it was Bear. He was a young man who stood at six feet five and tipped the scales at well over three hundred pounds. He was by far the largest man on the reserve. His size and nature had earned him the nickname "Teddy Bear." But on this night, his words were heavily slurred, and even the darkness could not hide the fact that he was staggeringly drunk.

What poured from his mouth impacted us like raw sewage. His normally quiet and respectful manner had been altered by drink into a raging torrent of profanities. He was backlit by a single yellow bulb from a distant house. His ominous outline revealed that he was carrying something, perhaps a board or a rifle. Not needing any more information, we quietly jogged the remaining distance to our little home.

Once inside, we locked the door and left the light off. In the darkness, we got ready for bed. But before we could settle in, we heard huge fists pound against the door. Bear had followed us home and now was trying to gain entrance. During our orientation, in the event of an emergency we were instructed to contact a family of believers who lived near the border of the reserve. They had a landline phone—but they lived two and a half miles away.

Bear's frustration increased with each passing minute that we refused to open the door. The pounding and kicking against the dilapidated door grew so violent that we were not sure how much longer it would hold. His spewing profanities escalated into a shouting narrative of all the things he was going to do to us once he broke through. The thundering fists and bellowing chronicles nearly deafened us to our own thoughts.

I looked at Beth through the darkness and nodded my head toward the giant opening next to the door. She looked at it. Instantly, her eyes widened in silent acknowledgment. The five-by-six-foot window opening that had been used for years as the only entry into our house was only covered by flimsy plastic vegetable bags taped together. All Bear had to do was move two feet to the right and he could step straight through.

In the deafening blackness, I reached for Beth's hands. Together, we knelt on the floor and prayed. The sewage bellow streaming outside was drowned out by the powerful prayer streaming inside. The brilliant name of Jesus poured into the shack and spiritual darkness was scattered. The redeeming blood that Jesus shed on the cross was acknowledged over our hearts, lives and circumstance. We asked that His glory would flood the environment around us. Fear was overwhelmed by faith in His presence. What tried to destroy us was itself destroyed. Our Defender was present and all fear was extinguished by the flame of His glory. We knew the Bear at our door was about to meet the Lion of Judah!

The pounding, screaming, kicking and shouting continued. The vile gush of hideous and repulsive words polluted the night.

But . . . the stars never stopped worshiping. And neither did we.

Through what felt like a disproportionately long time, the bellowing changed. After a while, it turned into elevated talking that declined into whimpering. The whimpering deteriorated into crying. The crying completely dissolved into silence. We heard our attacker stumble away. He did not return that night—or any night thereafter.

We were strategically placed to bring Jesus' message of hope, and we were not budging—it was the enemy who had to leave. This is the stance of His courage.

Joshua 1:9 says, "This is my command—be strong and courageous! Do not be afraid or discouraged. For the LORD your God is with you wherever you go."

Friend, the truth is this: When we are in the center of *His* will for our life, we are more safe in a plastic-bag shack besieged by a drunk in the wilderness than we are in our fortified homes surrounded by an army in a city. Our God is with us wherever we go.

No matter what we face, God the Father, Jesus the Son and the Holy Spirit are with us.

So does that mean we will never suffer? Not at all. It means that we can trust Him to be with us through every challenge we will ever face.

Isaiah 43:1–3 explains even further:

> But now, O Jacob, listen to the LORD who created you. O Israel, the one who formed you says, "Do not be afraid, for I have ransomed you. I have called you by name; you are mine. When you go through deep waters, I will be with you. When you go through rivers of difficulty, you will not drown. When you walk through the fire of oppression, you will not be burned up; the flames will not consume you. For I am the LORD, your God, the Holy One of Israel, your Savior."

As believers, we are going to encounter deep waters. We are going to encounter rivers of difficulty. We are going to walk through the fire of oppression. And our God will be at our side every step of the way.

Courage is the understanding that it is better to be anywhere uncomfortable *with* Jesus than to be anywhere comfortable *without* Him.

When we willingly position our hearts within His—no matter what circumstances we are in—this is where everything that He is becomes ours. His love, His joy, His peace, His patience, His kindness, His goodness, His faithfulness, His gentleness and His self-control flood into our soul, resembling rich golden oil. And in this place, there is peace.

Like a two-edged sword, the courage and peace of our God cannot be separated. The courage of our King is always peaceful. And the peace of our King is always courageous. When we truly have His courage, we will always have His peace—in any situation.

Jesus said to His disciples, "I have told you all this so that you may have peace in me. Here on earth you will have many trials and sorrows. But take heart, because I have overcome the world" (John 16:33).

No matter what we face in this world, we can choose to stand within the peace that Jesus offers. Standing in His peace is where "taking heart" or courage is forged. And we can rest in His courage because we know that He has already overcome every challenge that we will ever face.

I have heard it said, "You cannot worry and believe."

The enemy's singular desire for believers is the destruction of our faith, which separates us from our heavenly Father. Among the weapons in his arsenal of heavy artillery is fear. If the enemy's lies can create a barrier of fear within us, we will not move forward in courage. We will not trust God. We will not enter into the depth of His plan or presence.

When we are scared, this is how the enemy wins.

We will live our days cowering in an ineffectual corner, while crying out to God for help.

Our fear is tissue-paper thin. One single courageous act will carry us through its false walls of power.

Therefore, since we are surrounded by such a huge crowd of witnesses to the life of faith, let us strip off every weight that slows us down, especially the sin that so easily trips us up. And let us run with endurance the race God has set before us. We do this by *keeping our eyes on Jesus*, the champion who initiates and perfects our faith.

Hebrews 12:1–2, emphasis added

Fear confines those who obey it into a dungeon of futility in which the lying drone of "cannot" drowns out all other voices—especially God's beckon of "can." Those who obey the lies of fear often sense they are trapped in a black tunnel. They can see light in the distance; they can hear the deafening roar of an innumerable crowd.

The truth is this: The throng you hear is the "huge crowd of witnesses" (v. 1). They are cheering for you. With the fullness of their every breath, they are urging you to complete your part of what they have started. The completion of all believers' work will not happen—until you choose to run through the confinement of the tunnel and burst through the sphere and onto the field.

This is what reinforced courage looks like.

It hears God the Father leading the cheering roar. It hears Jesus call from the battlefield. It senses the Holy Spirit burning within, urging you to run to the front line. It acknowledges the long dark tunnel of fear leading to the field. It stares at the swirling black chains, moving like evil serpents, looking for any limb to confine.

Courage rises.

It leans against the black restraints, and they instantly snap.

Courage runs toward the light.

It draws closer to the colored sphere, and for the first time, you can see that the multicolored wall is only paper. With a single glorious leap, courage bursts through and into the brilliance of the Son. The huge crowd of witnesses goes wild with encouragement as another son, another daughter of the King has entered the realm of running the cross of Jesus Christ forward—no matter what the cost.

My beloved sister Chris recently shared the impacting poem "Afraid? Of What?" with me. Written by E. H. Hamilton, it inspired missionaries John Stam and his wife, Betty, before they were martyred in China for sharing the Gospel. It speaks of the courage that comes from *knowing* our true reward.

Jesus, because You did not back down from the cross to give me life, I will not back down from life to give the world Your cross.

This is courage revived . . . because this is the courage of our God.

Jesus,

Without courage, Your message through me will remain silent. So I give you all the paper chains of my fear. Over all other things, Jesus, reinforce my courage in You alone.

How can I read Your Word, proclaiming over and over that my heavenly Dad, Jesus and the Holy Spirit are with me wherever I go, and still choose fear?

When I'm scared, this is how the enemy wins.

It is a lie to keep thinking I can worry and believe at the same time.

Right now, I acknowledge that my fear is tissue-paper thin—one courageous act will carry me straight on through.

My Savior, as I give You all the construction paper chains of my fear, one by one, I call them out by name. And by name, I command them into the all-consuming fire of Your presence.

Today, I choose discomfort with You over counterfeit comfort without You.

I acknowledge that I will go through deep waters. I will pass through rivers of difficulty. I will encounter the fires of oppression. And You, my Father-Son-Holy Spirit, will be with me every step of the way!

My heart will not be afraid, even if I am attacked. I will remain confident in whatever "plastic shack" You call me to. No matter what "bear" attacks, I stand peaceful in the truth that it is the Lion of Judah who stands at my side.

Today, over all other things, Jesus, reinforce my courage in You alone.

Savior, with my hand in Yours, let's run!

I love You with my life.

Amen.

THIRTEEN

Reinforce My Stand

*Jesus, You are King, and I will not allow the
enemy to intimidate me with his lies any
longer—I choose to stand in Your authority.*

"The ruler of this world . . . has no power over me."

John 14:30

I had been contacted to be the speaker at a women's conference. As is our way, Judy joined me in preparation by fasting and praying specifically over this event. It was our fervent request before God that everyone present would be impacted and transformed by a head-on collision with the Father's love.

On the last day, I was preparing to impart the final message, the personal commissioning of each woman. As the ladies filed into the room, amid the crowd, a woman pulled me aside and shared some "interesting" news. She had just learned that among those attending the conference were four individuals who were deeply entrenched in the occult. Their sole purpose for coming to the event was to disrupt the gathering and attempt to stop the message of the Gospel of Jesus Christ from being spoken.

The courier who brought the news looked terrified. My first thought about the threat was to make a joke about duct tape, but the fear in the messenger's eyes conveyed that she did not need humor—she needed courage. I leveled my gaze directly at her face and replied, "Stand firm. Jesus is *way* bigger. Pray."

Around us, the auditorium was filling with the noisy fun energy of the ladies as they funneled in. Judy and I greeted many while finding a few empty seats in nearly the back row. We filed about halfway across the room and sat down. I was excited for what I believed Jesus wanted me to share with these women. As always, my heart reveled in the awesome privilege of getting to speak the message of His saving redemption—our daily growing relationship with Him—and our responsibility of love given back to Him.

As usual, the room filled from the front to the back. Judy and I purposely chose to sit behind the gathering so I would not disrupt anyone when I went to the stage. Also, from this position Judy was free to move about the back of the auditorium and pray. We were sitting nearly as far behind the assembly as we could get when a small group of women caught my attention. They also moved as far back in the room as they could go. With silent intention, the four of them filed into the empty row directly in front of Judy and me.

Often body language roars more loudly than words. In what appeared to be a shouting declaration from the leader of the quartet, she glared intentionally at my face before sitting in the chair right in front of me. Everything about her posturing seemed to declare, *You're not the boss here—I am!* Those following the lead woman silently sat to one side of her. She was much taller than the others and carried herself with a notable air of authority. Together, they formed an effective wall that cut us off from the rest of the room.

Completely sequestered behind the human wall, I was left to consider her silent roar. My quick conclusion was, *Hmm, you're partially right and completely wrong. You're correct in that I'm not the boss here. And you're completely wrong in that you're not either . . . because Jesus is!*

Seated directly in front of me, it was hard to not notice the leader. She had longish black hair that hung straight down her back. She was a relatively large-bodied woman with broad tanned shoulders that protruded well beyond the limits of her loose-fitting tank top. Simply because I could not see beyond her, I could not help but take notice of her movements. They were mechanical, even deliberate. With slow, dramatic premeditation, she reached behind her head, grasped the length of her dark hair with her right hand and pulled it completely over her right shoulder so her wide back was uncovered. Then, she leaned forward enough to pull her tank top down hard so the skin of her entire upper back was exposed. Leaning back as close to my face as her chair would allow, her intention was clear.

A huge black tattoo covered her upper back. Pushed to within inches of my face was hideous artwork that depicted a blood-drenched demon bursting through her skin. The creature's mouth was open, its fangs bared, its claws reaching—for me. I could feel my eyebrows move upward, externally saying what I was internally hearing, *Well, you don't see that every day.* My beloved friend Judy simply looked at me once and got up. Knowing this prayer ninja as I do, I had full understanding that she was not retreating—she was advancing.

Intimidation is the counterfeit shield of a fearful bully.

Judy stepped out of our row, filed into their row and sat right next to the leader. Then, my fearless, faithful, Jonathan-like friend reached into her spiritual arsenal of warfare and withdrew her mightiest weapon—the love of Jesus.

From any other perspective, what followed looked like a simple, beautiful conversation of one woman reaching out to another. But from my vantage point, what I witnessed was anything but. The leader was clearly rankled that Judy was not afraid of her. She appeared to be uncomfortable that her intimidation campaign had no effect on this quiet warrior bearing Jesus' love. When Judy welcomed the leader with a thoughtfully placed hand on her back, she nearly jumped out of the same skin that, moments earlier, she intentionally wanted us to see.

Truly, in every battle, spiritual or otherwise, Jesus' love wins every war.

This woman's blatant intimidation was easily crushed by the love of Jesus. The three "students" watched their leader's every move. Not knowing what else to do in front of her protégé, the leader chose to save what little control she had and ignore the kind woman closely seated on her left.

Wanting to stay focused on what was most important, I stood up and moved to the back of the room to pray. Meanwhile, Judy held fast—seated right next to the one who potentially needed Jesus' love the most.

Then my name was called, signaling it was my time to speak, so I moved through the auditorium and up onto the stage.

Not surprisingly, everything Jesus wanted me to share encircled the truth that if we call ourselves by His beautiful name, we carry the Spirit of the living God within us. Because we are bearers of His Spirit, we carry the most powerful spiritual weapon known to mankind—the redeeming love of Jesus Christ.

Fear has no place within the heart of any believer. Why? Because His "perfect love expels all fear," and this perfect love is God Himself (see 1 John 4:16–18). When God's people truly know who they are in Him and who He is in them, something beautifully powerful happens. When we understand even a portion of the ferocious, uncontainable love that we carry, the proof of this awareness will pour from us as we walk through this life in fear of nothing at all.

As I spoke from the stage, I noticed movement in the back of the room. The leader was shifting her weight from side to side in an obvious and odd way.

Undeterred, I pressed in with what He wanted me to share. Jesus did not leave us defenseless. He proclaimed in John 14 that He will not leave us as orphans in this world. No, He will come to us and live within us through the infilling of His Holy Spirit. With the full arsenal of everything the Holy Spirit brings—"love, joy, peace, patience, kindness, goodness, faithfulness, gentleness, and self-control"—believers are fully and lethally locked and loaded (Galatians 5:22–23).

With such a darkness-crushing arsenal within, all those who call themselves a Christian are already equipped to walk through any circumstance while carrying the light of our Savior. "The light shines in the darkness, and the darkness can *never* extinguish it" (John 1:5, emphasis added).

Again, I saw the tall woman in the back of the room waving her hands in front of her chest. Her fingers were bent in grotesque shapes. Over and over, she looked as if she were trying to throw something from her contorted hands toward me.

As part of the commissioning, I encouraged those in the auditorium who did not know Jesus as their Lord—or who once knew Him but had wandered from His grace or who knew Him well and were exhausted from the fight—to all stand up. It was time for each woman to take personal responsibility for what existed between her heart and the King of kings. It was time to honestly face the only One who could make right what was hurting and broken within.

The incantations and gyrations from the back continued. But they were not powerful enough to stop the message of hope from roaring into the room—or from one of her own three students from standing up to receive it. One of the "witches in training" encountered the almighty love of Jesus, and in that moment, the black chains of her darkness were not strong enough to restrain her honest reach for Jesus' love as she rose to her feet.

With her hands clutched tightly together under her chin, line for repeated line, she asked Jesus Christ to become her Lord. Nearly baptized by a flood of her own tears, her hands flattened against her chest as she privately proclaimed, *This heart now belongs to Jesus.* When the call was given for anyone desiring to be filled with the Spirit of the living God to simply raise their hands and ask Him, slowly she lifted her shaking hands from her chest and raised her palms up in humility, positioned to receive. Reaching for all she could, she received all that He gave.

This precious lamb was caught in the snare of the enemy's false arguments and empty promises of power, purpose and position. She was imprisoned by her own human reasoning and her own lack of understanding. But the mighty weapons of God's love walked right into her darkness, broke off her bondage and walked her right out and into the Kingdom of the Bright Morning Star—as a new daughter, friend, bride.

Light does not stay segregated or confined into a portion of space. Rather, it instantly permeates every realm into which it is released. When we release the light of Jesus into the environments we occupy, His powerful love cannot be confined or stopped. His loving presence rushes forward and transforms every heart that welcomes Him.

Consequently, when we encounter darkness, and step backward, darkness advances and swells into the vacuum we were meant to defend. When we confront our enemy, ours is not to struggle, fret or retreat into the caverns of our humanity and hide in fear. Instead, our highest calling is to step aside and allow darkness to run headfirst into the Rock of Jesus' love. Upon such no blackness can endure.

What shall we say about such wonderful things as these? If God is for us, who can ever be against us? Since he did not spare even his own Son but gave him up for us all, won't he also give us everything else? *Who dares accuse us whom God has chosen for his own? No one*—for God himself has given us right standing with himself. Who then will condemn us? No one—for Christ Jesus died for us and was raised to life for us, and he is sitting in the place of honor at God's right hand, pleading for us. Can anything ever separate us from Christ's love? Does it mean he no longer loves us if we have trouble or calamity, or are persecuted, or hungry, or destitute, or in danger, or threatened with death? . . . No, *despite all these things, overwhelming victory is ours through Christ, who loved us.* And I am convinced that nothing can ever separate us from God's love. Neither death nor life, neither angels nor demons, neither our fears for today nor our worries about tomorrow—not even the powers of hell can separate us from God's love. No power in the sky above or in the earth below—indeed, *nothing in all creation will ever be able to separate us from the love of God that is revealed in Christ Jesus our Lord.*

Romans 8:31–35, 37–39, emphasis added

When we stand up and humbly swing the almighty sword of Jesus' love, it will be the enemy who will run from all that abides within you and rushes from you. "So humble yourselves before God. Resist the devil, and he will flee from you. Come close to God, and God will come close to you" (James 4:7–8).

When we choose to come close to our God, He will come closer to us. The closer we are together with Him, the more the enemy will run from His presence that pours over, in and through us. The enemy does not run from us—he runs from God in us. The more of God's presence we carry, the more the enemy fears what we carry—and how we release what we carry through our voice of testifying about what He has done for us.

"And *they have defeated him* by the blood of the Lamb and *by their testimony*. And they did not love their lives so much that they were afraid to die" (Revelation 12:11, emphasis added).

Satan is defeated by the blood of the Lamb and the word of our testimony. James 4:7 declares that if we stand firm and hold our ground, our enemy will be defeated and destroyed by the power of God through those who bear His presence into the world.

"I have told you all this so that you may have peace in me. Here on earth you will have many trials and sorrows. But take heart, because I have overcome the world" (John 16:33).

Indeed, we will face hard things. But Jesus has already overcome every challenge, trial and sorrow that we will ever face in this world. He is already the victor. And when we truly believe this fact, we will be victorious as well. Friend, know this: The enemy might start the fight, but make no mistake—Jesus Christ always finishes it!

"We are human, but we don't wage war as humans do. We use God's mighty weapons, not worldly weapons, to knock down the strongholds of human reasoning and to destroy false arguments" (2 Corinthians 10:3–4).

Beloved, it is time for all who call themselves by Jesus' beautiful name to stop running away from the battle . . . and start running toward it.

Elijah stepped toward the prophets of Baal and they were incinerated (see 1 Kings 18). David stepped toward Goliath, the giant of the enemy camp, thereby destroying him and routing the army (see 1 Samuel 17). King Jehoshaphat stepped toward the advancing enemy armies and they were annihilated by the power of worship (see 2 Chronicles 20). Jesus exampled this in John 18:4: When faced with the cross, He stepped *toward* the enemy—not away.

Jesus stepped forward into that which He dreaded for one reason only . . . He loved and believed His Father more. Jesus did not step around or away from the will of the Father. Rather,

He stepped toward the cross, endured it and broke the power of death, thereby redeeming us. Complete redemption for all mankind—this is the priceless treasure we carry.

Now is the time to stand in this truth.

Jesus said, "I don't have much more time to talk to you, because the ruler of this world approaches. *He has no power over me*" (John 14:30, emphasis added).

We cannot allow our redemption to be stolen, stopped or derailed within our hearts through the deception of the enemies of the cross. No work of the enemy can undo or overwhelm Jesus' love. The enemy has no power over Jesus, and when His Spirit fills you, the enemy has no power over you either. Today, choose to stand in His authority.

Precious Savior,

You are King, and I will not allow the enemy to intimidate me with his lies any longer. I choose to stand in Your authority.

The enemy has no power over You, and when I am standing in Your presence, he has no power over me either.

The enemy's intimidation is only the counterfeit shield of a fearful bully—a bully who knows he has already been defeated.

The flaming missiles of fear shot from the enemy have no place within my heart.

When I resist him, when I stand in the power of Your love, he will run from me.

Jesus, I acknowledge the truth of John 1:5 that proclaims Your light "shines in the darkness, and the darkness can never extinguish it"!

Savior, it is Your love, shining through the darkness, that wins every war.

It is time for me to stop running from the battle . . . and start running to it.

Ignite my heart to fear no evil. Galvanize my strength to carry forward Your all-powerful love into the darkness.

Today, I choose to stand on the truth that the enemy might start the fight, but You, Jesus, always finish it!

Savior, open my eyes to the precious power of what I carry for You. Your loving redemption for all mankind is the priceless treasure You've called me to bear forth into the world.

Your redemption for all—this is worth standing for.

All for the love of Jesus.

Amen.

FOURTEEN

Reinforce My Discernment

*Jesus, reinforce my discernment as I listen intently
to Your words over the voices in my midst.*

Dear friends, *do not believe everyone who claims to speak
by the Spirit.* You must *test them to see if the spirit they
have comes from God.* . . . If a person claiming to be a
prophet acknowledges that Jesus Christ came in a real
body, that person has the Spirit of God. But if someone
claims to be a prophet and does not acknowledge the
truth about Jesus, that person is not from God. . . . But
you belong to God, my dear children. You have already
won a victory over those people, because the Spirit who
lives in you is greater than the spirit who lives in the world.

1 John 4:1–4, emphasis added

Once again, I had been invited to speak at one of my all-
time favorite churches. This unique body resonates with
my heart because it was one of the first places where I tangibly
experienced the presence of the Holy Spirit. Since that profound
moment, I have since realized that wherever the presence of

the living God is poured out, there you will also always find a frenzied swirl of the enemy. His sole purpose is to confuse by counterfeit. What the enemy does and says through misguided people looks and sounds like truth, but when followed to its conclusion, what they proclaim leads *away* from the unshakable truth of God's Word and the powerful love of Jesus Christ.

It had already been a glorious day. The energy and powerful moving of the Holy Spirit was evidenced by transformed lives. Many had chosen to stop focusing on their pain and start focusing on their King. By inviting His Spirit into their hurting places, many were filled with the glory of God in those same places. Their pain incinerated as their broken circumstances recalibrated before the love of the Father and their hearts were rebalanced on the truth of His Word.

The second service was emptying out, and those coming for the third service were making their way into the large sanctuary. Energetic worship music was streaming through the sound system with such volume that the walls themselves were vibrating with praise. I was standing between the front row and the expansive stage, surrounded by old and new friends, when a man approached me.

Instantly, even before he started to speak, I was aware that all was not well with him. He moved in an awkward and affected way, carrying his limp hands in front of his chest. He was shorter than me, heavyset, and looked to be middle-aged. When he started to speak, I had trouble hearing him. Between the loud, welcoming music and his heavy accent, I struggled to understand what he was saying.

Leaning in close, I asked, "How are you, brother?"

In a nearly mechanical way, he repeated the same line over and over. "I'm very sick. I'm in constant pain. I'm dying from what I face. I want you to pray for me to get well."

I was almost having to lip-read, so I leaned even closer and placed my hand on his shoulder to move my ear nearer to his monotone voice. The moment my hand settled on his shoulder, the Holy Spirit spoke clearly, *He does not know Me.* Intrigued, I pressed in by asking, "So . . . you know Jesus as your Lord and Savior?"

His expression flickered a nearly imperceptible flash of annoyance as he answered in a completely flatlined tone, "Yes-Jesus-is-Lord-and-Savior." What burned into my mind is what he did *not* say. He did not say "my" Lord and Savior.

Again, I pursued the truth. "I love hearing how people come to know the saving grace of Jesus. Please tell me how you came to know Him."

Again, the annoyed flash preceded his words. His account meandered out into the weeds with the identical speed of his English, both completely falling apart. In seconds, I could no longer understand him.

The worship team filled the stage and the third service began. We were standing feet in front of a massive sound system that was leading the entire large assembly into the worship song "Fierce" by Jesus Culture.

Amid the swell of rousing song, the small man in front of me circled back around and droned, "I'm very sick. I'm in constant pain. I'm dying from what I face. I want you to pray for me to get well."

Nodding in agreement, I stepped in even closer so that my lips were only inches from his ear, and his only inches from mine. With my hand still on his shoulder, I started to pray. The Holy Spirit highlighted that this soul did not know Him, so I began my prayer with praise and adoration and affirming Jesus' Lordship. Pure-hearted gratitude streamed from my lips directly into his ears.

That is when I heard something from his lips slam into my ears.

The man who only moments earlier struggled to speak English was now speaking perfect English. What he said was unmistakable. "I'm not leaving. I'm not leaving." His teeth ground together and he seethed again, "I'm not leaving! This is my home! I'm *not leaving!*"

This is what the Holy Spirit wanted me to know.

I pulled back just enough to look directly into the man's eyes. They were nearly black and unblinking—wild and . . . afraid.

Still holding his gaze, I moved my right hand from his shoulder to the middle of his chest, directly over his heart. Without missing a beat, my prayer shifted from affirming Jesus' Lordship to proclaiming His authority. "By the power of the name of Jesus and by the power of the blood He shed on the cross for this son, I command you to leave. You are trespassing in the heart of a lamb of God. I rebuke you! Get out! *Get out now!*"

The man took a sharp step backward, nearly falling in the process.

I followed him with my hand anchored over his heart.

His eyes closed tightly and his face contorted into an expression of excruciating pain. A sound started to stream from his mouth. It was the voice of an infant crying, identical to a tiny baby. Intuitively, I sensed this tormenting spirit had been harming him from early childhood. His cry intensified into a scream. His screaming grew louder and louder until it could be heard over the worship music. Then it transformed into a guttural, growling screech that was no longer human.

Startled by the awful sound, many around us moved away.

But many more moved in.

With hands on shoulders, all reaching forward toward a son who needed freedom, the body of Jesus Christ waged holy war—and prayed together amid the rousing chorus of "Fierce," a song that proclaims our Lord's powerful and pursuant love for the lost.

Indeed, the love of Jesus is fierce. For only a ferocious love would choose to leave heaven, walk among men, endure the cross and rise again to break the power of the enemy and our sin.

The shrieking ceased, and the man nearly collapsed into the arms of those who rushed to his aid. The hands that once hung limp before his chest were now alternately patting the place over his heart. A quiet, growing proclamation streamed over his lips. "Jesus is here. Jesus is here! Jesus is in my heart! Jesus is in my heart, and He is my Lord and Savior! Jesus is *my* Lord and Savior!"

There was no fight. There was no counter-attack. There was no debate. When it comes to Jesus' power versus our enemy's power, there is only utter defeat. Our Lord's commands are true.

> "These miraculous signs will accompany those who believe: They will cast out demons in my name. . . . They will be able to place their hands on the sick, and they will be healed." . . . And the disciples went everywhere and preached, and the Lord worked through them, confirming what they said by many miraculous signs.
>
> Mark 16:17–18, 20

On the heels of his tormentor's eviction, the man prayed a simple but direct, clarifying prayer of who his Lord really is— Jesus Christ. Nearly before he was finished praying, he shared that he had to quickly go and find his wife so she could also know the true, complete healing and freedom of Jesus Christ. Like those in the gospels who encountered the Author of genuine love, he ran back to those he loved and brought them to the wellspring of Jesus' love.

A truly changed life will result in a life that has truly changed direction.

In praying through the aftermath of the encounter, I realized how close I came to missing the entire point. The man asked me to pray for the healing of his body. But Jesus wanted me to pray for the healing of his heart.

How many times have I walked right by Jesus' perfect will because I was not fully listening to His voice spoken through the Holy Spirit? How many times have I prayed over the "sparks" blowing off the fire of the enemy within the heart of another when all along Jesus wanted to douse his evil blaze by sending in His unstoppable tsunami of living water?

Second Corinthians 11:14 warns that our enemy presents himself as an "angel of light." I have seen this evidenced throughout my time in ministry in that *all* those who had demonic oppression or possession told me they were believers in Jesus, except one. Many were employed by churches or working in high positions within ministries. And the enemy just laughs as he leads us away from the true cause, his horrific entrenched presence, which is destroying those in our midst.

The enemy hides behind half-truths. Indeed, this man was suffering physically. So often we automatically turn to the channels of knowledge that make sense to our humanity, those we easily understand, instead of following the Holy Spirit where He wants to go. What was causing this quiet man's suffering was not going to be healed through secular counseling, therapy, group sessions or any other human-based wisdom.

"Give us aid against the enemy, for human help is worthless. With God we will gain the victory, and he will trample down our enemies" (Psalm 60:11–12 NIV).

This precious man was not my enemy—what was residing within him was. Big difference!

"Now Christ has gone to heaven. He is seated in the place of honor next to God, and *all the angels and authorities and powers accept his authority*" (1 Peter 3:22, emphasis added).

Since all spiritual angels, authorities and powers accept His authority, is it not time that we accept it, too? Is it not time that we stop leaning into what we already know and start leaning into what we say we believe?

Friend, genuine discernment begins with genuine listening.

> But you have received the Holy Spirit, and he lives within you, so you don't need anyone to teach you what is true. For *the Spirit teaches you everything you need to know*, and what he teaches is true—it is not a lie. So just as he has taught you, remain in fellowship with Christ.
>
> 1 John 2:27, emphasis added

Indeed, following the leadership of the Holy Spirit while remaining in fellowship with Jesus Christ—this is the very definition of discernment.

Simply praying for this man to feel better would have been similar to what was happening in Ezekiel chapter 8. God speaks to the prophet of how the people look like they are worshiping Him, but hidden inside the temple, they were worshiping idols. From the outside, they appeared righteous. But deep within their hearts they had turned away from God and toward the enemy.

This is where genuine discernment is necessary. How things sound and appear might appeal to the pride of humanity. But appearances are meaningless to God.

His passion is for us to pursue all of Him with all that we are. Only making the outside look righteous is pharisaical, hypocritical, religious. Jesus despises fake religion so much that He saved His most angry verbal assault for such as these. In Matthew 23:13–33, the King of kings describes spiritual posers with words like hypocrites, blind guides, blind fools, sons of hell, filthy, greedy, self-indulgent, murderers, snakes and sons of vipers. Jesus was so angry at their prideful fake religiosity that in this single challenge, His passion warranted seventeen exclamation points—*seventeen*.

Jesus despises our pretending.

He did not endure the cross so we could pretend to belong to Him and pretend to be filled with His presence. Nor did He endure the cross so we could pretend to pray for sparks when He gave His life to extinguish, crush, obliterate the enemy's destructive fire.

True discernment is going after the flame that destroys—and destroying it with the *inferno* of our Father's love. Discernment is loving God by honestly listening to His voice of how to profoundly love His kids.

It is time to stop simply praying over the "sparks" of those who are hurting in our midst. Today is the day to start listening to the voice of the Holy Spirit. He is the One who leads into all truth (John 16:13). If we want the truth, we must follow His voice. We must step forward in faith and carry out what He desires.

This is His love. This is His discernment.

A hurting man asked me to pray that his body would get better. Jesus wanted to make all of him better. Jesus did not want to heal, redeem and free part of his heart. Jesus came to heal, redeem and free all of our hearts. He will do this for anyone who desires it wholeheartedly.

Our God is calling each of us to pursue Him into the deeper water of listening for His voice. Here, in the depths of His presence, discernment is found.

Precious Lord,
   The foundation of discernment begins with listening.
   I cannot discern what is true . . . if I am not listening to the voice of truth.
   Genuine discernment begins with listening to Your Spirit—the One who leads into all truth.
   Discernment that comes from You is loving—it goes after the fire that destroys the hearts of men.

Jesus, I don't want to miss praying over the removal of the enemy's fire, because I was deceived into focusing only on the superficial sparks.

Savior, when You reveal the enemy, I will not move Your love away. I will move Your love toward his stronghold, because true discernment doesn't settle for healing part of a heart—it presses beyond the surface into healing the whole heart.

Jesus, today, I purpose to listen beyond what is spoken on the surface to the powerful voice of Your Spirit. I ask You to help me practice becoming a John 10 lamb that knows the voice of Your Spirit and follows You where You want to go, because You will always lead straight into Your loving freedom.

Thank You, Jesus, for Your truth—truth that leads to redemption.

You are just so good, my Savior.

I love You.

Amen.

REIGNITE MY LOVE FOR THE LOST

Jesus replied, "The most important commandment is this: 'Listen, O Israel! The LORD our God is the one and only LORD. And you must love the LORD your God with all your heart, all your soul, all your mind, and all your strength.' The second is equally important: *'Love your neighbor as yourself.'* No other commandment is greater than these."

Mark 12:29–31, emphasis added

FIFTEEN

Reignite My Testimony

*Jesus, may my testimony be reignited by walking
in the authority of what You have done in my life.*

Jesus came and told his disciples, "I have been given all
authority in heaven and on earth. Therefore, go and make
disciples of all the nations, baptizing them in the name of
the Father and the Son and the Holy Spirit. Teach these
new disciples to obey all the commands I have given you.
And be sure of this: I am with you always, even to the
end of the age."

Matthew 28:18–20

I had been summoned to teach at a prestigious Christian university in the eastern United States. A portion of what I was
called to do was encourage their entire student body during a
university-wide service.

The chapel was stunning. Built in the early twentieth century,
it reflected the architectural splendor and detail of that era. All
the wood was dark and ornate. The windows featured glorious
stained-glass imagery of Jesus' journey of faith. The elegant

stage was high and surrounded by opulent floor seating that was augmented with a second deck of balcony seats. Surrounding the base of the platform were cushioned kneeling benches. The wall behind the podium was nearly concealed by an enormous pipe organ, the biggest I had ever seen. Within this place of worship, one could feel the deep, drenching faith of the decades.

My admiration was abruptly cut short by a young producer assigned to instruct me on the exact flow of events. I was informed where I would sit, how I would sit, when to stand, where to walk and where to look. The normal fifteen-minute message slot was stretched to eighteen minutes to allow me more time to encourage the student body and staff.

I was also informed this was "prospective week," the time frame in which potential students come with their families to evaluate the university for future enrollment. Because of the large wave of possible new students, a sense of urgency and excitement rippled among the faculty.

Soon, the stately old chapel filled with wave after wave of young and old. As the students, faculty, visitors and families filed in, the atmosphere began to change. Instead of feeling vibrant with life, I sensed something else. The climate in the room transferred from profound reverence to something that felt more like . . . a pause, a "check the box," a duty.

No matter. Aware of the shift, my job and my joy remained the same. In minutes, a young worship team filled the stage and played their previously allotted two worship songs with skill and energy. After a few announcements and an encouraging word from a student, the guest speaker was introduced. I walked across the stage to the podium.

My view from this hallowed position was magnificent. Spread before me were several thousand faces, a literal human tapestry of cultures, races, religions—all blending together in a unique and awe-inspiring mix. I wondered how heaven could be more beautiful.

Rising like an internal upside-down waterfall, the presence of the Holy Spirit surged forward in a geyser of enthusiasm, hope and love. I did not know what the audience expected to hear; I was only aware of what the Holy Spirit wanted to say. He is the One who leads into all truth (see John 16:13). His love crashes through our "boxes," obliterates our "duty" and speaks the redeeming power of the Gospel of Jesus Christ.

Beginning in a familiar way, I shared how everyone comes from somewhere, everyone has survived something. We all have a history, a foundation from which our journey of faith begins. I recounted how at nine years of age, I thought my mom was the most beautiful woman on earth, and I wanted to grow up and be just like her, especially on the inside. My dad was an outdoor enthusiast. Aside from his primary job, he was also a downhill ski instructor on Mount Shasta. He taught me how to ski when I was four. My family lived near Whiskeytown Lake, located in the far-northern reaches of California. With such close proximity to this gem, my dad also taught me how to waterski when I was four. At the ripe age of five, my adventure-loving dad pulled me up my first mountain, a local 10,463-foot volcano called Mount Lassen. To escape the perpetual summit winds, we nestled down together behind a makeshift rock wall. From beneath his arm, I watched cloud spindles form right in front of us, dance across the pinnacle and then vanish over our heads. My life has never been the same—I have lived in a permanent love affair with the mountains ever since.

During that time in my life, I knew there was nothing my dad could not do. In my eyes, he was a superhero. I also believed that he wore an invisible cape and could fly. Cradled between my mother's gentle love and my dad's passion for adventure, my life was perfect . . . until it was not.

Within this season, my dad's best friend came to my school and picked me up. He pointed for me to sit behind him in his car while he retrieved my two older sisters. Lined up across the back seat, the three of us drove in silence over a familiar road that led to our grandparents' home. Without words, each of us experienced the crushing, choking sense that something horrific had happened. My oldest sister was sitting next to me. For solace, I glanced up at her face, which by then was streaked with silent tears. Not knowing what to do, I stared out the window and wished I was in the mountains.

Suddenly, from my position at the podium, I heard a commotion in the audience. I glanced up and saw activity up in the balcony to my right. It came from a distinguished group of students I had met earlier who were visiting from Africa. Even from my distance, I could easily identify them by their distinctive red Maasai clothing draped royally across one shoulder. There were maybe eight of them, and they were leaning together and all talking at once in their native language.

From across the aisle a beautiful dark-complexioned woman rose and went to them. The Maasai students all moved toward her and spoke in excited tones. I saw her point at me and make some gestures with her hands. Then she sat down on the floor in the aisle next to them and they quieted.

Whiplashing back to my journey of faith, I pressed on. Once we turned down the long driveway that led to my grandparents' house, I could see random cars parked in disarray. When our car came to a stop, I could not move. I could not breathe. For the first time in my young life, I did not want to enter a house where I only ever experienced love—I was afraid.

Someone pushed me inside through the wailing crowd and into the arms of a woman I vaguely recognized. She was crying so hard that she could scarcely breathe. She kept circling in a sickening spiral of sobbing and gasping amid the words, "I'm sorry . . . I'm sorry . . . I'm so, so sorry." Finally, she broke. "I'm so sorry. I don't know how to tell you this . . . but your father has just murdered your mother and then taken his own life . . . I'm so sorry."

Worlds collided.

What she said and what I knew did not line up. In my world, my dad loved my mom, and he loved me, and he would never do that. I shouted in her face, "Liar!" Then I broke out of her arms and bolted out the back door. I ran a short distance that felt like miles and finally collapsed into the freshly tilled earth of a tiny orchard.

Lying facedown in the dirt, I grasped handfuls of soil. I could hear myself sobbing, inhaling dirt, choking, coughing and retching. Then, in the odd silence that followed, I heard what I thought were animal sounds. I did not even recognize the tone of my own voice when I started to plead, *Jesus . . . Jesus, help me . . . help me . . . I need You now.*

At that time in my life, I did not even know who Jesus was. I had not been raised in the Church. All I really knew about Jesus was that I was pretty sure He was the guy on the cross. But in that moment of mortal crushing, I was certain He was the only One who could help me. I did not know God's Word or verses like Romans 10:13 that proclaim, "Everyone"—*everyone*—"who calls on the name of the LORD will be saved." I had no idea that Romans 10:9–10 (ESV) promises, "If you confess with your mouth that Jesus is Lord and believe in your heart that God raised him from the dead, you will be saved. For with the heart one believes and is justified, and with the mouth one confesses and is saved."

All I really knew in that moment was this: I was no longer alone and I felt a "pop" in my heart. An ignition of hope had begun, a growing sense that *somehow* I would survive this—I would make it through. Perhaps from somewhere high above, angels watched as Jesus Christ came and knelt in the dirt beside a breaking child. He took the tiny hand that was reaching out for Him . . . and He has never let go. Not then. Not now. Not ever!

In the darkest moment of my life, I called Jesus' name, and the Lord of loving hope came into my heart. And He has never left.

In the season that followed, it was His love that redeemed and healed the devastation within my heart. It was His hope that drew me forward into wholeness. It was His peace that quieted the storms of grief, and it was His joy that filled my heart then and floods it to this day.

I relayed how Jesus takes the events with which our enemy means to destroy us and transforms them into the very thing that gives us life—only He can do that.

Indeed, our pain has a purpose. All of it. If we do not believe this, it only means we have not yet turned the corner into trusting in Him more than our pain.

This is what Jesus can do with pain, any pain, given to Him.

When we surrender our suffering to Him, He makes it into something beautiful, powerful, life changing. But there is something He cannot heal—the pain we refuse to give to Him. And this is pain that destroys.

Pausing for a moment, I looked out across the sea of faces before me. They were completely still, silent, listening, grappling. Many were weeping. Some were sitting with their elbows on their knees, holding their heads, looking straight down.

It was time to throw the life ring.

I reminded the assembly of Jesus' all-consuming love for each one of them and the power of Matthew 11:28, where He encourages burdened hearts to come to Him. I invited anyone who wanted to receive the healing hope of Jesus to symbolically leave their place of pain behind and come forward to receive His outpouring of loving redemption.

What started out as a trickle quickly turned into a flood.

Swollen rivers of hurting hearts crushed forward to repent, acknowledge Jesus Christ as their Lord and receive Him as Savior. Within the throng of those who wanted to pray, I met a lovely dark-complexioned woman named Mya. She spoke softly with a distinctive African accent. She recounted how she had come to this university independently to research it for her potential future. Once I started to speak, she heard excited voices arise across the aisle to her left.

The commotion was from the Maasai contingent, a culture she was not familiar with. To her astonished amazement, as she *listened* to them, she realized she recognized their every word. She clearly heard how they were frustrated because they had come so far and wanted to understand what the speaker was saying, but there was no one who could translate for them.

In bewildered awe, Mya shared, "I didn't know I could translate the Maasai language—until this moment." Two heavy streaks ran down her face. "The . . . the things I heard myself telling them . . . the love and hope of Jesus? I didn't know that He can forgive me. I didn't know that He can heal my heart. I didn't know that He . . . that . . . He loved me so much." The fragile dam that held back her emotions completely caved in beneath the rushing tide of her tears. Truth was breaking through.

Kneeling by her side, I cradled her as she wept.

As her torrent of tears began to subside, she whispered, "Do you think He . . . He might . . . receive someone like me?"

Gently, I placed my curved index finger under her chin. "Look at me."

Gradually, the tumble of wavy black hair lifted away from my shoulder as she lifted her head. The gaze of her deep-brown eyes slowly rose and leveled with mine.

"Beloved," I began, "He would've come if it was only for you. He loves you so much. It was His Spirit that opened your mind to understand a language you do not know. So *He* could translate His love into your heart. So you would know." I paused. "Mya, would you like to ask Jesus to be the King of your life today? If you ask Him to, He will forgive your sin, heal your brokenness and fill your heart with His joy. Do you want the gift of His love?"

With our eyes still locked, a fresh flood streamed down my friend's beautiful face as she nodded. Completely washed in a cleansing of her own tears, Mya's heartfelt cry of repentance, her desire to receive Jesus' love and her streaming gratitude converged into one of the most beautiful prayers I have ever heard.

And just like that, a stunning African woman ran and jumped into the arms of the One who loves her most.

And just like that, His words, through you, can do the same.

The power of the Gospel impacts every life that truly has ears to hear.

Words have power. When we choose to yield our words to the loving leadership of the Holy Spirit, our words carry His eternal life-giving power. This is why Jesus gave all believers the Great Commission, which is so important that it was recorded in all four of the gospels:

> "I have been given all authority in heaven and on earth. There-fore, go and make disciples of all the nations, baptizing them in the name of the Father and the Son and the Holy Spirit."
>
> Matthew 28:18–19

> "Go into all the world and preach the Good News to everyone."
>
> Mark 16:15

> "Yes, it was written long ago that the Messiah would suffer and die and rise from the dead on the third day. It was also writ-ten that this message would be proclaimed in the authority of his name to all the nations, beginning in Jerusalem: 'There is forgiveness of sins for all who repent.' You are witnesses of all these things."
>
> Luke 24:46–48

"Peace be with you. As the Father has sent me, so I am sending you." Then he breathed on them and said, "Receive the Holy Spirit."

John 20:21–22

Genuine revival is always fueled by love. God's love for us was expressed through the sacrifice of His Son so we could be redeemed, filled with His Spirit and live with Him forever. Jesus asks us to express our love in return by telling the world about His saving grace.

Although this calling has not changed, for many, the personal application has. Multitudes have succumbed to the slippery slope of compromise and no longer believe the fullness of this command applies to them. Today, through man-made religion, the Great Commission often looks more like the "great comfort."

"These people honor me with their lips, but their hearts are far from me. Their worship is a farce, for they teach man-made ideas as commands from God" (Matthew 15:8–9; see also Isaiah 29:13).

It is true that Jesus came into this world to ease our pain, sorrow and suffering. But this is only a portion of why He came. With these beautiful gifts comes equally beautiful responsibility. Jesus Christ gave His life to enact the Great Commission in every believer's life—my life and *your* life.

"Prove by the way you live that you have repented of your sins and turned to God. Don't just say to each other . . ." (Luke 3:8).

We must break through our pride, fear and complacency and pursue His will deep into the loving realm of sharing His abundant hope, joy and love. *This* is what transforms the broken in our midst. When our hearts are genuinely filled with Him, He is what comes out. Our testimony of what His love has done within us becomes the flashpoint that ignites healing redemption in the hearts of people around us who are dying without hope.

God's Word is filled with examples of this phenomenon: In Mark 5:3–18 Jesus casts out a legion of demons from a man roaming in a cemetery. He is so filled with gratitude that he begs Jesus to go with Him. Jesus tells him, "No, go home to your family, and tell them everything the Lord has done for you and how merciful he has been" (v. 19).

Friend, for most, ministry begins in our home.

"So the man started off to visit the Ten Towns of that region and began to proclaim the great things Jesus had done for him; and everyone was amazed at what he told them" (v. 20). His life was instantly transformed, and instantly, he set out to tell others what Jesus had done for him.

In John chapter 9 Jesus heals a man of lifelong blindness. Immediately after he was healed, he began praising God. And when he was pressured by religious leaders to denounce Jesus, he instead testified of what Jesus did for him (see vv. 26–33). Genuine redemption produces genuine gratitude. And genuine gratitude transforms the heart it lives within.

When the disciples were filled with the Holy Spirit in Acts chapter 2, they immediately began sharing the Gospel, and the early Church was formed by the spoken word of their testimony.

This is the power of our testimony. When we release what Jesus' powerful love has done in our life, we literally bring God's will from heaven to earth. By releasing God's authority into the realm of men, the power of Satan is completely defeated.

> Then I heard a loud voice shouting across the heavens, "It has come at last—salvation and power and the Kingdom of our God, and the authority of his Christ. For the accuser of our brothers and sisters has been thrown down to earth—the one who accuses them before our God day and night. And *they have defeated him by the blood of the Lamb and by their testimony.*

And they did not love their lives so much that they were afraid to die."

Revelation 12:10–11, emphasis added

Friend, when you speak of what Jesus has done in your life, His love through you demolishes enemy lines, breaks off the enemy's power and sets the captives free. This is what Jesus does through any life that steps forward into the Great Commission and speaks out His redeeming love.

Out of our hearts come our words. So what is in your heart? Are your words driving others away from His hope—or drawing them toward it?

Jesus said, "Let the dead bury their own dead, but you go and proclaim the kingdom of God" (Luke 9:60 NIV).

Now is the time to choose. Your life can only go in one of two directions: You can spend it "burying the dead" or you can "proclaim the kingdom of God."

Jesus Christ's voice rings with equal power today as it did for the apostle Paul when He said, "Don't be afraid! *Speak out! Don't be silent!* For I am with you" (Acts 18:9–10, emphasis added).

Because He has redeemed you, may you choose His love to flood your heart. May today be the day that *His* voice through you is reawakened.

"But to all who believed him and accepted him, he gave the right to become *children of God*" (John 1:12, emphasis added).

Beloved, your words are powerful.

His truth, spoken through your lips, opens the doors for those in your midst to become children of God.

Our Lord is not asking that we fulfill the "Great Suggestion"; He is commanding us to fulfill the Great Commission.

Jesus is calling each of us to speak in such a way that those who know you, but do not know God, will come to know God *because* they know you. This is the reawakening of your testimony.

Ask Jesus to revive the most powerful thing that you will *ever* speak. Ask Him to revive your declaration . . . and start speaking out all that He has done for you.

Jesus, words are *powerful.*

Today I call You my Lord because someone spoke Your love to me.

I acknowledge that millions of believers throughout history have died so the baton of Your salvation could be run forward and placed into my hands.

It was not for the "Great Suggestion" that they gave their lives, but for the Great Commission.

Now, this sacred commissioning has been handed to me.

Today, I carry You, the Hope of nations, within.

In this moment, I willingly lay down every barrier that has sealed my lips—lips Your love has already released.

May my gratitude compel me to share Your hope with anyone You highlight.

Right now, I commit to run forward Your baton of love in any way You desire.

I ask that You use this vessel to pour Your love into the atmosphere of men—that more will know of Your saving grace.

Jesus, today, *I commit my every word to be used for Kingdom purposes.*

Reawaken my testimony for Your glory!

Amen.

SIXTEEN

Reignite Your Spirit within Me

*Jesus, it is my desperate desire to experience the
full reignition of Your Holy Spirit within me.*

"And I will ask the Father, and he will give you another
Advocate, who will never leave you. He is the Holy Spirit,
who leads into all truth. The world cannot receive him,
because it isn't looking for him and doesn't recognize
him. But you know him, because he lives with you now
and later will be in you."

John 14:16–17

The roar from the engine of our Alaskan bush plane overwhelmed our ability to speak. But that did not stop Troy
and me from squeezing each other's hand when we saw something beautiful, which was every second that our eyes were
open.

He squeezed my hand and pointed down. I leaned over his
lap and looked in the direction he indicated. Below, a herd of

caribou trotted across the tundra. Next, I squeezed and pointed at several massive caribou bulls bedded down together by a lake. Troy nearly crushed my hand with excitement when he saw a gigantic brown bear sow with her three cubs in tow.

We had been gifted a coho salmon fly fishing adventure in the unspoiled wilds of the Alaskan Aleutian chain. The fishing and guide counsel had been so stellar that even a beginner fly fisherman such as myself had already caught the outer limits of believability. As if to add a definitive exclamation point to the trip, we were now flying out to a remote river that empties dramatically into the Bering Sea.

Nothing made from the hands of men could be seen in any direction. No roads or villages existed in this wild place. The nearest town was Cold Bay, 180 miles to our southwest. Nothing lay in between but tundra and sea. Like the plane we flew within, my heart soared, completely lifted by the absolute power and raw beauty of this place. I could literally see my God's peace, His authority, His enduring love reflected in everything that filled my senses.

Our highly skilled pilot lowered the plane to within feet of a desolate dark-gray beach. I presumed he was scanning it for landing suitability. It was steep and strewn with wooden debris and salmon carcasses. As I was silently agreeing that it would be impossible to land there, he touched down the uphill wheel and rode it like a kid doing a two-hundred-yard wheelie. As the plane slowed in the loose sand, the rest of the landing gear contacted the beach, lurching us all downhill toward the ocean.

Once our plane came to a rest, I ripped off my pilot communication headset and nearly flew out the tiny door. I wanted to laugh. I wanted to scream. I wanted to do cartwheels down a wild beach. I did not think my heart could hold any more thrill for life.

But I was wrong.

With all our gear tossed in a heap onto the sand, our intrepid guide and two beloved friends, along with Troy and me, all waved at our pilot as he zoomed out of sight into the vast expanse of the Alaskan sky. The drone of the plane was immediately overwhelmed by the music of the wilderness. Our hearts flooded with the sounds of a wild sea and wind in the grass. Without thought, I joined in creation's song and started to sing worship to the Maker of all.

Soon, our little group had transported our gear the short distance to a powerful waterway called North Creek. We spread out along and within the river. The wild silence was punctuated by our whoops, cheers and laughter as one salmon after another was reeled in and carefully released back into its watery home. Throughout the day, our revelries were slowly replaced by a profound, silent reverence.

During our brief lunch break, each expressed a nearly tearful awe of gratefulness. God Himself was in this place. We could feel His presence. We could feel His unfathomable love. Before Him, we were overcome with wordless gratitude.

After lunch, I felt a draw as familiar as my own heartbeat—a deep beckoning to walk in the wild . . . with my God.

Since the beach was covered with brown-bear tracks, our treasured guide and I scrambled up the highest grassy dune to scout for stragglers. The elevated vantage point allowed us to see about a mile and a half down the beach. Once he felt the way was safe, and I promised to go no farther, he released me to adventure alone.

In minutes, I set out over sand as dark as an eagle's wing. Instantly, my heart filled with the wonder that few, if any, human feet had tread this lost stretch of surf. The only way in was by plane, at low tide, and with favorable weather and a relatively clear beach.

Drawn into the embrace of the wild, I walked with my arms loose at my sides, palms forward, praises pouring from my lips.

Completely removed from the influence and distraction of humanity, my heart swelled into the space, the sacred expanse of His presence. Tears of wonder, worship and gratitude streamed down my face. I pondered if heaven itself had touched earth in this beautiful, powerful, holy moment.

I had walked to the near limit of which I had promised. Still lost in the glory of the scene, movement caught my eye. It was to my left, up the beach toward the grassy dunes. Suddenly, my heart shifted into high alert. In this place devoid of humanity, I realized that I was no longer alone. I stood fast and surveyed the environment. Just below the grass and coastal brush lay a massive tangle of driftwood. I studied it, looking for anything that could be a threat.

Frozen in place, I waited as long moments passed. Adrenaline filled my body. I could hear my heartbeat.

Then, from behind a log, the identity of the wild resident was revealed.

A red fox appeared.

We held each other's gaze, each measuring the intention of the other. Growing up as a girl of the wild places, I wanted to engage this beautiful masterpiece. To convey I was no threat, I dropped my eyes and started to move slightly away from the fox. Carefully, I walked up into the grass and sat down, purposefully looking away. To my absolute delight, the fox jumped up on a log, walked its length *toward me* and then stepped down into some shrubbery and curled up. We were only yards apart.

I guessed he was a lone male. Mesmerized, I admired his every detail. His eyes were brilliant gold, rimmed in coal black with nearly vertical pupils. His intelligent, upright ears moved to catch any whisper of sound. His top line was coated in bright red, and beginning around his black nose, white extended across the lower half of his cheeks, down his chest and spread over his belly. His legs were black. His paws seemed large for his size, clearly designed for traversing boggy tundra and snow. His downy tail with a white tip appeared to be nearly equal to the size of his entire body. After lying down, he had wrapped his tail around himself and nestled his chin into the lavish pillow.

Appearing refreshed by the brief rest, he trotted down to the beach and consumed a washed-up salmon carcass. I "casually" pursued him and sat down on the sand not far from where he had enjoyed his meal. He stared at me for a long moment, again seeming to measure my intentions. I purposefully looked away and shifted my weight. While still watching me intently, he lay down on the beach.

What happened next was one of the most endearing wilderness encounters I have ever experienced.

Satisfied that I was no threat, the fox relaxed and stretched out his front legs. Following his lead, I did the exact same thing. Yellow eyes searched green eyes. With our inquisitive gazes still locked, the fox playfully tossed his chin up. I did the same thing. Next, he opened his mouth and completely rolled over on his back, white belly toward the sky. Again, I mirrored his every move. My little red friend continued to roll from side to side. He stretched his front paws toward me. He lay flat on his belly with hind legs stretched behind, *all the while* watching me. In return, I imitated his every gesture, *all the while* watching him. This sweet engagement continued, blurring the confinements of time.

Forged with the same clarity and power as the wild that surrounded us, an "invitation" was being fashioned.

Intrigued, the fox rose to his feet and started to carefully circle me. I held fast. As he moved past my shoulder and beyond my view, I did not turn around. In a wilderness demonstration of trust, I allowed, even invited, complete vulnerability. Not wanting to miss a thing, I carefully held up my cell phone so I could see what was transpiring behind me. To my astonished delight, the fox approached to within feet of me. There he stopped, stretched out his neck as far as it would reach and explored the scent of my back.

Knowing a flinch would send my new friend into flight, I sat completely motionless. I was nearly holding my breath, as I did not want the moment to end. On a desolate beach embraced by the Bering Sea, a wild fox was invited to encounter a wild-hearted woman.

Once his curiosity was fulfilled, the fox pulled back a few yards and sat down again. Only vaguely aware that I was smiling, he appeared to have accepted me into his "pack."

Needing to return as promised, I finally had to get up and start moving back toward my own pack. As I stood up, my red friend did not leave or advance. He merely watched.

While retracing my tracks back to the others, I had time to reflect.

Wow, God! I'm astounded at what just happened. Please speak Your truth over this encounter and open my eyes to help me see what You see.

I remain so profoundly grateful that Jesus used parables to show us things we can see and understand—to illustrate things we cannot yet see and are trying to understand.

Days later, some unique truth did come when I shared the wilderness encounter with my dear friend Judy.

Her quiet observation landed on my heart with all the subtlety of a lightning strike. "Wasn't that fox just like the Holy Spirit?"

Pure clarity poured over the scene.

"So if you sinful people know how to give good gifts to your children, how much more will your heavenly Father *give the Holy Spirit to those who ask Him*" (Luke 11:13, emphasis added).

I do not know how long the fox was present with me in the wilderness, perhaps the entire hike. But this I do know: He did not approach until he was "asked." I needed to purposefully offer an invitation, a literal and physical "welcoming" for him to come. I had to stop all movement and be still. I had to wait. I had to be quiet. Only then did he come.

◆ ◆ ◆

Our heavenly Father wants to give the Holy Spirit, *His* Spirit, to anyone who "welcomes" Him.

Consider Cornelius in Acts chapter 10. He was a devout man who loved God, gave generously to the poor and prayed regularly. But he was still devoid of God's Spirit. Until he stopped intentionally. Until he purposed to be still. Until he waited. Until he stopped everything and welcomed the presence of the Holy Spirit inside the home of his heart.

Only when Cornelius asked God for more of His presence did more presence of His Spirit come.

Our God has not changed (see Hebrews 13:8). The Holy Spirit of our living God desired a welcoming, a literal invitation then, and He desires the same today . . . with everyone who calls Him Lord.

When I was nine, I had an encounter with Jesus Christ on the day of my parents' death. I was aware of His presence and love but still did not know Him. It was not until a year later that I formally asked Jesus to come into my heart and be my Lord and Savior. Following that simple prayer, as the Lord of all accepted the invitation to come into my life, something else also came in. In that hallowed moment, a single line, one sentence of unknown phrasing also joined the King as He took His rightful place in my heart.

This string of sounds remained firmly embedded in my heart. During times of crushing, fear, elation or praise, they would stream to the surface like holy music coming from a place beyond my understanding. It was always the same sentence followed by the same word that repeated three times at the end.

Perhaps because of my conservative upbringing and lack of comprehension, only a few times did I ever mention this curious phenomenon. Each time it was dismissed by spiritual leaders as being self-invented or emotionally dangerous, verging on the loss of control. From childhood to adulthood, I was firmly taught to believe in the Father, Son and Holy . . . book. The Holy Spirit was only mentioned in passing.

My upbringing intimated that you could not trust the Holy Spirit, because He might ask you to do something uncomfortable, hard, scary or, worst of all, embarrassing. So to avoid discomfort, fear and embarrassment, I learned to disregard His presence.

But His presence did not disregard me.

Just like the fox on the beach, His presence was always with me, shadowing my every move, waiting for the simple welcoming, the invitation to lead.

For years, I did not invite Him. In fact, I did the opposite. I discounted and judged those who chose to follow His beautiful voice. I viewed them as spiritual "thrill seekers" who valued emotionalism more than God. I relegated their fantastic accounts of God's presence breaking into the realm of men as exaggerated stories shared only to gain attention. I did not believe them or their accounts, because I had never experienced what they spoke of. So I assumed it could not be real.

But the Spirit-given phrase embedded in my heart *was* real—and it would not be silent.

In contrast, I wholeheartedly believed God's Word was real. After reading through the gospels and Acts, again and again, and examining all the amazing signs and wonders, I could not dismiss Jesus Himself saying,

> "I tell you the truth, anyone who believes in me will do the same works I have done, and even greater works, because I am going to be with the Father. You can ask for anything in my name,

and I will do it, so that the Son can bring glory to the Father. Yes, ask me for anything in my name, and I will do it!

"If you love me, obey my commandments. And I will ask the Father, and he will give you another Advocate, who will never leave you. He is the Holy Spirit, who leads into all truth."

John 14:12–17

I wanted the truth!

By pouring through the Word that I knew was true, I discovered one fact after another.

- "Do not stifle the Holy Spirit" (1 Thessalonians 5:19).
- "Do not bring sorrow to God's Holy Spirit by the way you live. Remember, he has identified you as his own, guaranteeing that you will be saved on the day of redemption" (Ephesians 4:30).
- Peter and the apostles said, "We are witnesses of these things and so is the Holy Spirit, who is given by God to those who obey him" (Acts 5:32).
- Jesus said, "I tell you the truth, all sin and blasphemy can be forgiven, but anyone who blasphemes the Holy Spirit will never be forgiven. This is a sin with eternal consequences" (Mark 3:28–29).

My questions started to circle around this reality: If the only unforgivable sin is to blaspheme the Holy Spirit, then why in Christianity is the Holy Spirit so maligned and misunderstood? Why are believers so afraid of Him? Why do we struggle so mightily with receiving and relying on His presence?

The answer was obvious. In order for anyone to truly receive and follow Him, they must willingly give up their perception of control.

He wanted me to give Him my control.

The Holy Spirit is God. He is an equal part of the Trinity—Father, Son, Holy Spirit. And yet by discounting Him, I had effectively removed one of the legs of His three-legged stool and was trying to balance my understanding, my faith, my ministry, my life on only the two supports of three that I honestly believed.

I clearly saw that what I was doing looked and sounded good, but it was nearly powerless. In effect, the cables were all in place, the fuse box was hooked up and ready to go, but I still had not flipped the switch of the Holy Spirit to the On position. There was no power in the cables.

Since, I have heard the beloved Reinhard Bonnke say, "When it comes to the Holy Spirit, He is the electricity in the cable. You will not know that there is power in the cable . . . until you touch it."

I knew about the cable but had not yet dared to touch it.

Until I did.

In that moment I reached, asking the Holy Spirit to *fill this life* with everything that He is, and I grabbed the cable of His presence with both hands. And nothing about this life has ever been the same. His brilliant glory flooded in and consumed what I thought was light.

Jesus said, "Make sure that the light you think you have is not actually darkness" (Luke 11:35).

I did not know what I did not yet have. Nor could I fathom the difference. Then suddenly, verses like Luke 5:36–39 made sense:

"No one tears a piece of cloth from a new garment and uses it to patch an old garment. For then the new garment would be ruined, and the new patch wouldn't even match the old garment.

"And no one puts new wine into old wineskins. For the new wine would burst the wineskins, spilling the wine and ruining the skins. New wine must be stored in new wineskins. But no one who drinks the old wine seems to want the new wine. 'The old is just fine,' they say."

Luke 5:37–39

I had been content with old wine and stuck in old faith—until I tasted the new wine. When His new wine began flooding this container, my old understanding burst on impact, unable to contain the sheer volume of His love, peace, patience, kindness, goodness, joy, gentleness, faithfulness and self-control—the fruit, the overflow that is Him (see Galatians 5:22–23).

My choice to limit my consumption to old wine resulted in old ministry. It was not until I tasted Him, truly drank deeply of His Spirit, that I understood the difference. It was not until I encouraged the Holy Spirit to pray through me that the single line given to me the day of my redemption streamed into His beautiful language.

"*Taste and see that the* LORD *is good.* Oh, the joys of those who take refuge in him!" (Psalm 34:8, emphasis added).

Our Lord is holding the cup of His Spirit to our lips and encouraging us to taste, try, consume, pursue. It was never His intention for us to simply know *about* His Spirit. He desires us to welcome Him into our hearts and experience all that He is. He wants us to actively pursue knowing Him, every day, and follow His lead.

1 John 2:27 assures us that the Holy Spirit teaches us everything, *everything*, we need to know. The Spirit of the living God is ready to offer you

- His direction and leadership[1]
- Sensitivity to His voice[2]

1. See Matthew 4:1; Mark 1:12; Luke 2:27; 4:1; Acts 8:29; Romans 8:14.
2. See Matthew 10:20; Acts 1:16; 2:4; 13:2; 28:25; Hebrews 3:7.

- His power to cast out demons[3]
- His anointing[4]
- His filling or baptism[5]
- His new birth[6]
- His worship[7]
- His truth[8]
- His strength[9]
- His view of the future[10]
- His gift of prayer and interceding[11]
- His dreams and visions[12]
- His guidance[13]
- His life[14]
- His fruit[15]
- His help[16]
- His witness[17]
- His adoption[18]
- His conviction[19]

3. See Matthew 12:28.
4. See Luke 4:18; Acts 10:38.
5. See Matthew 3:11; Mark 1:8; Luke 1:15, 41, 67; 3:16; 4:1; John 1:33; Acts 1:4–5; 2:4; 4:8, 31; 6:3, 5; 7:55; 10:47; 11:24; 13:9, 52; 1 Corinthians 12:13.
6. See John 3:5, 8.
7. See John 4:23.
8. See John 14:17; 15:26; 16:13.
9. See Acts 9:31; Ephesians 3:16.
10. See John 16:13.
11. See Acts 2:4; Romans 8:26–27.
12. See Acts 2:17, 18; 11:28.
13. See Mark 13:11; Acts 10:19; 11:12; 21:11; 1 Timothy 4:1.
14. See Romans 8:2, 10.
15. See Galatians 5:22–23; Ephesians 5:9.
16. See Romans 8:26.
17. See John 15:26; Acts 5:32; 15:28; 20:23; Romans 8:15–16; Hebrews 10:15; 1 John 4:13; 5:6–8.
18. See Romans 8:15.
19. See Romans 8:13; John 16:8.

- His miraculous power[20]
- His love[21]
- His revelation[22]
- His purity[23]
- His gifts[24]
- His sealing[25]
- His liberty[26]
- His access to God[27]
- His unity[28]
- His wine[29]
- His supply[30]
- His fellowship[31]
- His grace[32]
- His glory[33]
- His teaching[34]
- His boldness[35]
- His sight[36]

20. See Acts 1:8; 1 Corinthians 2:4.
21. See Romans 15:30.
22. See Luke 2:25; 1 Corinthians 2:10, 12; Ephesians 1:17–19; 3:5.
23. See Romans 15:16; 1 Corinthians 6:11; 2 Thessalonians 2:13; 2 Timothy 3:16; 1 Peter 1:2, 22.
24. See 1 Corinthians 12:4–11; Hebrews 2:4.
25. See 2 Corinthians 1:22; Ephesians 4:30.
26. See 2 Corinthians 3:17.
27. See Ephesians 2:18.
28. See Ephesians 4:3–4.
29. See Ephesians 5:18.
30. See Philippians 1:19.
31. See 2 Corinthians 13:14; Philippians 2:1.
32. See Hebrews 10:15–17, 29.
33. See 1 Peter 4:14.
34. See Luke 12:12; John 14:26; 1 Corinthians 2:13; 1 John 2:27.
35. See Acts 1:8; 4:31.
36. See Acts 9:17.

- His commission[37]
- His restraint[38]
- His ministry[39]
- His love[40]
- His joy[41]

Before God, is there a single soul who calls Jesus Lord who does not truly desire these things? This is the new wine the Holy Spirit offers to anyone who asks.

He also gives us His renewal.

> When God our Savior revealed his kindness and love, he saved us, not because of the righteous things we had done, but because of his mercy. *He washed away our sins, giving us a new birth and new life through the Holy Spirit.* He generously poured out the Spirit upon us through Jesus Christ our Savior.
>
> Titus 3:4–6, emphasis added

All these things, including a new birth and a new life, are being offered through the Holy Spirit *to you.*

Just like the captivating fox on the beach, the Holy Spirit waits for your invitation. The cable of God that connects His will being done here on earth as it is in heaven, the power source from the Father's heart to yours, is within your reach.

"Since we are living by the Spirit, let us follow the Spirit's leading in every part of our lives" (Galatians 5:25).

Beloved, *today* you can welcome His Spirit into the home of your heart.

37. See Acts 13:4.
38. See Acts 16:6.
39. See Acts 20:28.
40. See Romans 5:5.
41. See Romans 14:17; 15:13; 1 Thessalonians 1:6.

Lord Jesus,

Reignite Your Holy Spirit within me.

I'm sorry for being so consumed with the business of fulfilling the small picture that I've missed the big picture—the ultimate picture of positioning my heart purposefully, quietly to welcome and receive all that You desire to pour within me.

Jesus, thank You for giving clarity through a simple wilderness encounter.

Thank You for encouraging me to ask for the presence of Your Spirit.

Holy Spirit, I kneel before Your almighty presence today, and with my hands over my heart, I choose to stop, to wait, to be still. With full welcome, I invite You, Your very presence, to come into the home of my heart.

Please fill every inch of my being with the glory that is Your holy presence. I ask for Your love, Your joy, Your peace, Your patience, Your kindness, Your goodness, Your faithfulness, Your gentleness and Your self-control to become the living foundation stones within my heart.

Today, I commit to follow You in every part of my life.

Thank You, Father. Thank You, Son. Thank You, Holy Spirit for Your kind, gentle pursuit of my life. Thank You for never leaving me. Thank You for guiding me. Thank You for filling me. Thank You for loving me.

I love You in return with every beat of my heart.

Amen.

SEVENTEEN

Reignite My Will to Live for You

Jesus, may my passion for You burn with such unquenchable heat that it blazes through every barrier of my unwillingness until there is nothing left—except a heart ignited for You alone.

And so, dear brothers and sisters, I plead with you to give your bodies to God because of all he has done for you. Let them be a living and holy sacrifice—the kind he will find acceptable. This is truly the way to worship him. Don't copy the behavior and customs of this world, but *let God transform you into a new person by changing the way you think.* Then you will learn to know God's will for you, which is good and pleasing and perfect.

Romans 12:1–2, emphasis added

It was October 12. Although the day was sunny and beautiful, our sonar reported the incoming ocean water rushing beneath our boat was a chilly 49 degrees. Troy and I had been fishing our favorite place on the Coquille River, out on the bar. The locals call it "Jaws" because in this confluence, an outflowing river and an inrushing sea smash together in a crushing bite of colliding waves.

In this beautiful, turbulent place, I love to stand at the rail of our boat so I can fully experience the wave movement. Every swell has a face, a peak and a back. Each one comes, confronts your balance and goes. This reminds me to do the same thing in life. When confronted by the tumultuous waves of this world, if we maintain our stability in Jesus, our challenges will roll on by.

A licensed captain and fishing guide, Troy aligned our craft with skilled experience to glide up the face of each wave, then rock headfirst down the other side. Occasionally, the boat would pitch hard on the crest, as if it were falling. He would just laugh and say, "Wow! That one had some teeth!"

Our small vessel pitched and rocked for hours. I held my chosen post at the rail and allowed my body to sense and adapt to each new angle. Throughout the afternoon, the wind continued to build, pushing the waves into dangerously steep green folds. We fished in this place until it finally became too perilous to continue. With reluctance, we hauled up our fishing gear and headed upriver.

We passed the Harbor Masters building and Weber's Pier. Troy slowed our boat as we approached the entrance to the Bandon Boat Marina, where we had been mooring during our stay. Uncharacteristically, he asked if we should simply turn into the marina and end this beautiful, blustery day early. Troy had given nearly every day of his season to guide others, and with only two more days to fish, I wanted him to revel in every last glorious minute. High slack tide would be around three o'clock, so I encouraged him to point our boat upriver and fish out the last hours. Once we rounded the bend by Bullard's Beach Landing, the wind, blocked by the dunes, calmed a bit. We lowered our gear back into the depths and trolled upriver.

Within minutes, Troy caught a beautiful silver salmon buck. We made a few more lazy passes that all ended under the bridge. The river was now in a strong flush and pushing hard out to sea. Although the salmon fishing had been unusually poor, we were blessed with four takedowns and four beautiful silvers in the net. Gently, we returned each back into the river.

It was 4:15. We had finished a pass that ended above Bullard's Beach Landing. Troy looked at me and grinned. "I know it's getting late," he said. "Just one more pass. I want my bride to catch the last fish of the day."

Strangely, my normal "fish 'til dark" DNA faltered. I heard myself say, "Today's been incredible. I'm good to go in."

He joked that I must have hit my head or some other mishap that altered the synapse pathways in my brain. We laughed together and readied the boat to head in.

Within my heart, I noticed something that felt like an echo. Again, I sensed, *Good to go in . . . go in . . . go in now. Leave now! Go!*

From under the Coquille River bridge, with an unexplainable sense of urgency, we hauled up our tackle for the day. I stowed the gear on the boat as Troy brought up the trolling motor and put down the main. Once the main engine roared to life, Troy put it in gear and headed back toward the harbor.

It was about 4:30, and the river was a ghost town; the heavy wind drove the usual end-of-day boats home hours earlier. We streamed past Bullard's Landing and made a long sweeping bend to the left, which led into the wide wind-swept expanse that eventually leads back to the marina. I looked down the broad stretch of water before us. Here, the river opened to nearly a quarter mile wide of heavy wind-driven waves.

In the distance, something strange caught my eye.

There were bright colors in the main channel. I could not understand what my eyes were seeing. "Troy, what is that?" I asked.

He was also straining to make out what was ahead. Intuitively, he swerved toward the object. It was about fifty yards off the eastern shore, and from our distance appeared to be a multicolored mass of floating debris. Carefully, we slowed down to investigate. Closing the distance, Troy put the boat in neutral and let it drift close. I still could not make sense of what I was seeing, and then . . . it moved.

A man was in the water!

My brain jolted as the puzzle pieces crashed into place. What sprawled before me was a capsized boat. A man was drifting near the almost-submerged upside-down hull. He raised his arm weakly and rasped a barely audible, "Help me."

In a single motion, I retrieved our salmon net and held it as far over the starboard side as I could. "Grab it!" I shouted. "Reach! Reach for it!"

The man was elderly. He could barely move. His hands did not seem to work. He could not grasp the net. With one hand holding the boat railing, I lay flat on the side wall of our boat. By balancing completely on my hips, my feet left the floor and I lunged as far as I could reach. The man slowly moved his hand forward like a rigid hook. By Jesus' grace, he caught the rim of the net.

"Hold on!" I shouted.

Regaining my footing, I pulled him toward our boat. Among the floating debris, he was tangled in drifting loops of yellow rope. I followed the rope with my eyes. It was attached to his boat, which was now completely underwater. This man was entangled in rope that was connected to the sinking wreckage. In seconds, he would be pulled beneath the surface. My scrambling thoughts were crushed by a single deafening roar: *Get the ropes off him! Pull him in and free him—now!*

Fueled by urgency, I shouted, "Hold on! I've got you! I've *got* you! Hold on. You're gonna be okay . . . you're gonna be okay."

As I carefully guided the suffering man through the wreckage, his head lolled backward. Then, I heard him whisper, "But he's not."

What? My eyes darted through the wreckage.

Nothing.

I looked straight down into the space I was guiding him toward and realized I was dragging him directly into the body of a second man in the river. In that moment, all I could truly comprehend was that his face was in the water. "Jesus, help! Help us!" I yelled. "*Come now! We need you now! Jesus!*"

Troy lunged his upper body over the rail and caught the second man's life jacket and jerked him toward the boat. With the salmon net still in my hands, I drew my man to the back of the boat where the motor mount was. The diamond-plated mount was nearly level with the water and only one by two feet in size.

I jumped over the transom onto the mount and grabbed my man by the shoulders of his life jacket and pulled him to the mount. As he was losing consciousness, I shouted, "C'mon, c'mon! You can do this! Stay with me, sir. *Stay with me . . . Fight!*"

Waves battered us both as I fought to lift him onto the platform. Loops of yellow rope swirled around his legs. He was big-bodied, elderly and in the throes of lethal hypothermia. His eyes were unfocused. His face was white. His lips were blue. He could not help me. He was drifting deeper into unconsciousness.

Again, I cried out to Jesus. "Make me strong . . . Make me strong!"

Then I hauled backward as hard as I could. His chest came up onto the motor mount, and I caught the back of his pants. Crouching, through my clenched jaws, I could hear His name pouring out around me. Heaving to my feet, I felt a full-body electrocution.

The limp man's torso lifted in chorus with my straightening legs. As only Jesus can command, a strategically large wave slammed into the back of the boat. It rolled completely over the man and knocked me backward. But it also forced the man's knees to wash up under his chest onto the plate beneath us.

Again, I screamed.

Again, the electrocution of His presence.

Again, supernatural strength was given to lift a helpless man's chest high enough to slide onto the transom.

I jumped over the back of the boat and pulled him farther up so he was lying across the transom. Next, I scooped up his legs and spun him so they fell into the boat. Then, while throwing his limp arm across my shoulder, I heaved the rest of his body onto the bench seat.

"You're gonna be okay! You're gonna be okay! Everything is going to be all right," I said, perhaps trying to convince both of us at the same time.

He was mostly upright and shaking violently. His eyes were unfocused and his mouth was open. Prayer streamed from my lips. My thoughts bounced like a pinball back to my mountaineering search and rescue days. *His heavy shaking is good. His body is still fighting to make heat.*

Turning away from my man, I lunged headfirst over the rail to help Troy. He was still holding the second lifeless man next to the boat. Instinctively, Troy took a firm grip on his life vest; I followed his lead and gripped the man's belt.

Troy shouted, "Pull!"

Heaving with our combined strength, we could only lift him a few inches out of the water. His limp, soaking-wet body made him nearly impossible to grasp.

Again, "Pull!"

Over and over we tried to lift him into the boat. His life jacket tore apart, then slipped completely off. In quick succession, his belt snapped in half and his pants started to tear. We had nothing to hold him with.

"To the back!" my husband commanded.

We guided his body to the rear of the boat. Without letting go, Troy jumped over the transom and sat on the motor mount. With heavy waves breaking over them both, he quickly looped his arms under the lifeless man's arms and tried to wrap his legs around the man's large torso.

"Take us in! But go slow. I can barely hold him!"

Leaping to the helm, I put the main in gear, with full understanding that the spinning propeller blade was only inches away from the love of my life and a stranger in dire need. With utmost care, I slid the prow around and started to take us in. The harbor entrance was a quarter mile away.

Troy shouted, "I'm losing him! *I'm losing him . . . I can't hold on!*"

Leaving the main motor in its lowest gear, I ran to the back of the boat. Troy was fully sitting in the water and trying to hold onto the collapsing arms of the man who was slipping out of his grasp. Reaching over, I took the man by the wrists and heaved him back up into Troy's lap as my husband desperately sought to gain a better grip.

The current was so strong that the boat was instantly pulled off course. We were being dragged toward the ferocious waves of Jaws and toward the open ocean.

On this day, none of us will survive.

Running back to the helm, I corrected our course. Troy fought with a lion's heart to hold onto a man who, at the very least, was someone's son. Over and over, I ran between helping my husband hold onto a man in desperate need and steering the boat away from the sea and toward the marina.

At one point during the chaos, I called 911 and shared, in a hail of adrenalized words, that we had just pulled two men out of the river. One had severe hypothermia and the second had already drowned. "We're heading into the marina. We need help *now!*"

The skilled operator spoke calmly and directly. "Ma'am, please stay on the line."

Troy growled through his teeth as he fought with superhuman strength to hold onto an unconscious man being pulled from his grasp by horrific current.

Without thought, I tried to pass my phone to the other rescuee, but he was no longer conscious—nor was he shaking. His hypothermia was advancing into the red zone.

Clunk!

My phone fell to the floor behind me as I jumped over the transom to help Troy hold on. Suddenly, I heard a loud crunch, and Troy and I were pitched hard into the back of the transom. Again, the violent wind and current had shoved us off course and the bow of our boat had struck the large boulders that guard the marina entrance.

Once more, I dashed to the helm and took the boat out of gear. I shouted to my husband to stay clear of the prop, knowing that once I put it hard into reverse, it would draw everything close into the strong vortex of the propeller. The man was completely in the water. Troy's legs were less than a foot away.

"Clear the prop!" I yelled. Blinking away visions of amputation and surrounded by streams of unknown prayer language, I put the main engine into a hard reverse. The boat shuddered and dug deep against the current, then pulled free from the rocks. Spinning around, I noticed Troy was still upright and appeared to be okay.

With supernatural clarity, he told me to call the fuel dock on his phone. Our friend answered with her normal cheerful greeting. Instead of hearing the usual request for gas, she heard, "There's a drowned man on your fuel dock. Call 911. Come down and help me *now*!"

The fuel dock was now about twenty yards away. With the horrifying reality that men were in the water and nearly under the prop, I shut down the main engine and let the boat drift the remaining distance to the dock. Again, I rushed back to assist my husband.

Troy had gained enough grip to move half of the man's rib cage up onto the motor mount and was holding him with one hand while attempting one-armed chest compressions with the other.

I looked up to see the wind was blowing us away from the dock.

We were not going to make it.

I could not risk the men by starting the main engine again. I grabbed the end of the stern line, ran across the back of the boat and jumped off the rail toward the dock. The line drew taut in midair.

My shoulder whipped backward, and I felt my body spin around. Instead of landing in the water, my feet hit the edge of the fuel dock. Not expecting to hit wood, I collapsed hard on the wooden deck. I landed completely backward and was now in a crouched position.

I should not have made it.

Pulling the boat in, I tied the stern hard and fast to the dock, then glanced up to where our friend would typically appear to hand down the fuel nozzle.

No one.

Jumping back over the transom, Troy and I hauled the man's torso up onto the one-by-two-foot space of the motor mount. I knelt with my knees balanced between the main motor and the trolling motor with my legs in the sea. In this position, I could cradle the man's head in my arms. With no space to spare, I could not comprehend what Troy was standing on, but stand he did and was giving deep chest compressions.

Multiple sirens screamed past us.

I looked down. The man in my hands appeared to be about 75. His gray hair and full white beard stood out in shocking contrast against the purple pallor of his skin. Even in this surreal state, eyes closed and mouth open, his face bore an undeniable kindness.

We struggled to turn the man on his side so his lungs could drain. Turning him back to flat, Troy continued hard compressions. What had filled the drowned man's lungs and stomach was now coming out everywhere. Foam and vomit flooded my lap as I held his face in my hands.

Time froze.

A profound realization overwhelmed me: I was cradling the cheeks of a loved one. He was a son, perhaps a husband, an uncle, a brother, a father, a grandfather, a friend. This man was loved.

Then He spoke.

Kim, will you fight for him? Will you press into his chaos and do all you can to help him? Will you push past the ugliness of the moment and give him everything you have, whatever it takes to save him? If it were him holding your face, wouldn't you wish for the same?

Taking a deep breath, I wiped the vomit off his face, pinched his nose shut and sealed my lips over his. I blew hard into his mouth. My breath was met with equally hard resistance. What filled his lungs came spewing out into my mouth.

Moments lengthened into a monster that could not be satisfied. Again and again, I tried to fill his lungs with oxygen-laden breaths. Over and over, the response of his body was to divulge stomach contents that had been previously aspirated. Vomit filled my mouth and covered my face, chest and hands. I did my best to spit it out, press in, push through and pursue life.

I heard running steps on the dock. I looked up to see a young man dashing toward us. His expression was one of pure fear. He, too, was pressing in, pushing through and pursuing life.

I pointed at him and motioned to keep coming and jump into the boat. "Quick! Help us get him off the motor mount and onto the dock!"

Without explanation, we traded places as spinning lights of several rescue vehicles pulled up to the entrance of the marina. Help was here; they finally found us.

Jumping back over the transom and into the boat, I reengaged the man who was now slumped over on his side on the bench seat. After pushing him upright, I grabbed both of his wrists and stooped to look at him eye to eye. "Friend, you're gonna be okay."

His eyes were unblinking, vacant, lifeless, reflecting only that he was still unable to comprehend what was happening.

"Sir, sir, sir! Look at me . . . what's your name? What's your name?"

With my face a dozen inches in front of his, he blinked a few times.

"Sir, what's your name?"

Repeatedly, he moved his lips, attempting to form his name. But all he could manage was, "R-r-r-r." After several attempts, what finally shivered out was, "R-r-r-r . . . Ray."

"Ray! Let's get you out of these wet clothes." I took hold of his light blue shirt and ripped it straight up over his head. Shirt buttons pinged off the deck. In a single motion, I dried Ray's body and hair and then wrapped him in towels. He was too stiff to maneuver into Troy's heavy jacket, so I laid it over his shoulders. Next, I wrapped his head in another towel and pulled him into a strong, full body embrace. While hugging his back, shoulders, arms and head, I prayed in the Spirit over him.

A noisy commotion from behind pulled my glance back toward the dock—now filled with multiple first responders, shuffling, reaching, heaving, all trying to work in concert with Troy to move the drowned man onto the dock. Once the man was moved, a paramedic pressed in and began powerful chest compressions. I could hear the sickening sound of bones breaking as human ribs gave way. His shirt was cut off as the defibrillator was charging.

Over my shoulder came the ominous command, "Clear! Clear! Clear!"

Then I heard nothing. No adrenalized pursuit. No elation. No response. The beloved man with the kind expression and whose face I had been cradling was *dead*.

As I tightened my embrace around Ray, who was starting to shiver again, a stream of encouragements flowed from my lips: "You did good, Ray. You held on. You kept fighting. You did it. You're going to be okay. Everything is going to be all right."

The other man's body was placed onto a stretcher and covered, then wheeled away. I heard a police officer ask Troy, "So what was your friend's name?"

Troy's exhausted response was, "I-I don't know. We just came upon their capsized boat in the river. My wife and I just pulled them out of the water."

"Wha-what?" the officer said. "What do you mean 'them'?"

Troy pointed toward the helm of our boat, where I was warming Ray. "There were two men."

The officer whirled around. His sweeping gaze instantly measured the scene. He took notice of the disarray, the wet clothing on the floor of the boat, the violently shivering elderly man who was hastily wrapped in whatever dry materials were available—and the disheveled woman who enveloped him in the universal posture of giving her warmth. His gaze settled on my face . . . and his eyes softened.

Sitting down on the bench seat across from Ray, the compassionate officer asked him a hail of questions. Ray was blinking more, and his eyes were beginning to move. Slowly, he was regaining consciousness. Even still, he was largely unable to comprehend what was being asked of him. All that was truly determined was a single stunning fact: The men had been in the river for approximately an hour and a half at 49 degrees—thirty minutes beyond lethal for any human being.

Ray was still in dire need. With no other available ambulance in the small community, the officer elected to take him immediately to the hospital in his personal squad car. By draping our survivor's arms over each of our shoulders, the officer and I stood up and Ray hung suspended, trembling between us. Together, we eased him to the side of the boat. There, many hands reached down and four strong souls gently lifted him up onto the wooden platform and into the squad car. Still on the dock, Troy assisted them with all their gear, and as fast as they arrived, the first responders dashed away.

I stood alone in the boat.

I looked up at the fuel dock platform ten feet over my head. It was now lined with about sixty onlookers. I stared up at them; they stared down at me. I was vaguely aware that I still had vomit in my mouth and on my face and chest. One woman gave me a wordless thumbs-up and silently clapped, apparently applauding my effort to try to save another. I gazed at her and returned a mute shrug, communicating with equal silence that my efforts were useless because I did not reach him in time. And because of that single fact, a man lost his life.

My heart felt empty, numb.

Not really knowing what to do next, I reached for a water bottle and used it to rinse my face and mouth. I picked up one of the sopping towels from the floor and did my best to wipe off my chest. The whole moment felt surreal, like I was moving in slow motion.

Jesus, did that really just happen?

The boat shifted as Troy stepped down into the hull. I turned away from the onlookers and toward the human love of my life. Before I could reach for him, he was already reaching for me. Within the deafening quiet, we embraced for a long moment. I could feel him stroking the back of my head and kissing my brow. His silent affirmation spoke volumes that indeed, every moment of this life is so very precious.

The rest of the night was somber, a wordless swirl of imagery. I could not eat. I could not sleep. Instead, I lay awake in bed all night, grieving for the man who could not stop cataclysmic events and watched his best friend die. I grieved for the family that was experiencing the wrecking ball of sudden loss. I grieved over the fact that all my efforts to help revive someone's beloved son had been useless.

In the rolling waves of reliving sights, sounds and actions, a single question kept crashing against my heart: *Why, Jesus? Why would You save one but not the other? Even though one man had already died by the time we arrived, Lord, the water was cold. You could've revived him. Isn't that what You wanted? Jesus, he could have perished days before, and You still could've raised him back to life. Why, Lord? Why would You strategically position us to intervene . . . and only save one?*

In the early hours before dawn, my heavenly Father's voice began to quietly stream into my heart. There was an awareness, a subtle reminder of something Jesus said to Peter. It was something He said *after* a rebuke for Peter wanting his own way instead of trusting the Father. In response to my pleading, *But Jesus, weren't we there to be Your loving hands and feet and to save the men? My Savior, I was screaming for Your help, desperate for You to do what only You can. Why did You refuse to respond?*

Behind the rebuke of Matthew 16:23 rose the remainder of the verse: "*You are seeing things merely from a human point of view, not from God's.*" Again, He spoke.

Beloved daughter, you have been so focused on the single miracle you perceive that I did not do that you have failed to see the zillion miracles that I did do.

I gave you a boat. I equipped you to fish.

I sent you out on this precise day.

I gave you the power of My presence through the beauty and glory of My creation.

I sent the big wind and waves to move you upriver.

I delighted you with more fish.

I kept you upriver and moved you into the perfect position to carry out My plan. I told you when to return to the marina.

I opened your eyes to see what needed to be done. I prolonged a life.

I made your net handle longer to reach a man in need. I gave him the ability to hook the net.

I kept the other man afloat so you could bring him back to his family. I kept the boat from sinking and pulling the other man to his death.

I gave you supernatural strength. I sent the wave to help you.

I kept your husband and the man he held from being destroyed by the propeller. I gave your husband supernatural strength to hold onto a loved one. I protected them both the entire way.

When you jumped, it was I who caught and carried you to the fuel dock. It was I who was breathing through you.

I sent the young man to help.

It was My love within you that overcame adversity and saved a life.

Beloved, you are so focused on what you perceive I did not do—restore a life—that you have missed all that I did do. Your screams for help were to save a man's life. I have saved his life . . . just not in the way you expected.

I have answered your request with love beyond your ability to understand. What you perceive as the worst day of this man's life . . . is actually the best day.

Now My son is in My arms. He's home.

In the light of a new day, more miracles were revealed.

While drifting over the deep green waves of Jaws, Troy noticed a message on his phone. Putting it on speaker, we listened to it together.

The male voice was tentative and thin. "Hi, you don't know me . . . but I'm the man you pulled out of the river . . ." His voice trailed off, broken with emotion. "You saved my life . . . and I don't . . . I don't even know your names. Can I, can I . . . meet you somewhere? I want to thank you face-to-face . . . and . . . and . . . just give you a hug." Struggling to regain a small measure of composure, he continued, "I'm alive. Today, I'm alive . . . because of you. Thank you."

An hour later, we met on the dock. Two strangers fell into each other's arms and wept. This remains among the most profound embraces of my life.

We learned the timeline of when Ray was pulled from the icy waters until he reached the hospital was about an hour and a half. The attending physician declared that his core body temperature had warmed up to 90 degrees, which for most . . . is dead. He had *warmed up* to a temperature that was medically lethal! The doctor shared that he was a man of science and that he did not believe in miracles, but he found it hard to deny when he was standing there speaking to one. He told Ray that he had no medical explanation for why he was alive.

We also discovered after the boat capsized and the men were hanging on to the wreckage in the water, three boats—three—passed them and did not stop.

By the time Troy and I reached them, one man had already perished. All Ray could remember was hearing someone say, "I've got you . . . I've got you . . . you're gonna be okay." Then, he woke up in the hospital. Yet during that time, Ray described something astounding. From when he heard, "I've got you" until he was revived in the hospital, he experienced something astonishing. As he tried to find the words, his eyes flooded with tears. Finally, he explained, "I felt arms around me. I knew I was out of the water. But I still felt waves . . . waves of indescribable, uncontainable, unfathomable rollers of compassion. In a way I don't understand and cannot explain, I encountered the most powerful love I've ever experienced during a time of . . . death."

Flesh had encountered Spirit. This is our Father's love. It comes in uncontainable waves, and even death cannot stop it.

The worst destruction we will ever face in this world, when we look, is still saturated in the Father's love. All the deadly distractions of the enemy cannot change this fact. When we first discovered Ray, he was entangled in floating loops of yellow nylon rope. The line was fastened to crab pots that were secured to the boat, and the boat was already completely underwater. It was sinking. Ray was tangled in ropes connected to wreckage that was pulling him to his death. In about ninety seconds, he would have been dragged beneath the waves.

This is a clear picture of how our enemy works.

In Hebrews 12:1 we are commanded to strip off the entanglements of sin. It does not matter if the ropes are from your own wreckage or the wreckage of another, their insidious purpose is the same. Whether we are seeking help or giving help, this fact remains—the yellow lines will ensnare anyone who nears them. And without firm awareness that they are anchored to death, anyone who becomes entangled within them will be dragged down to destruction.

Understand this: All ropes are from the enemy. They appear as lazy loops of pride, fear, bitterness, complacency, immorality, guilt, unforgiveness. As harmless as they might first appear, all are connected to death; all pull toward annihilation. So when they appear, we must remove their authority by acknowledging, *Not my ropes, not my wreckage.*

Because Jesus died so I could live, I refuse to allow the enemy to entangle my heart, mind, soul and strength in loops anchored in the pit of hell. Instead, I will acknowledge their presence and steer clear. I will reach for those ensnared around me with the saving net of Jesus' love and draw them to the "rescue boat" that is my heavenly Dad.

"Dear brothers and sisters, if another believer is overcome by some sin, you who are godly should gently and humbly help that person back onto the right path. And *be careful not to fall into the same temptation yourself*" (Galatians 6:1, emphasis added).

Beloved, you exist in the world today for a reason. You are strategically placed by the Father for His great purpose—to love Him with all that you are and to reach the lost with His compassion. In this great river of life, there are people in the water all around you. In your midst, friends, co-workers, neighbors, family members are entangled in the deadly ropes of this world and are being dragged to their death.

Will you take your highest calling seriously? Will *you* reach out, with His love, to those in the water? Will your hands become the link of love that draws them toward salvation? Will you push through the circumstantial vomit, the ugliness meant to deter you and pursue life—their life in Jesus?

Serving our King was never meant to be about our comfort—but our commitment. As those who call ourselves by Jesus' name, we cannot keep driving by. We cannot smile and wave and hope the next boat of Christians will do something.

Jesus entered earth's atmosphere to break the power of sin and death and to set the captives free. Your greatest job, your highest joy is to introduce the drowning in your midst to the only One who can save them. It is the all-consuming love of Jesus that repels the entangling ropes of the enemy.

He showed us step for step how to do this—with His own life. He is not asking us; He is commanding us to do the same. As those who are called believers, we have been commanded to fulfill what Jesus started. He has fully equipped us with His name, His blood, His Word and His Spirit.

If Jesus is your Lord, you already have this arsenal at the ready. The real question is, Are *you* ready? Are you ready to trust Jesus more than your education, more than your experience, more than what you feel, more than what makes sense? Are you going to trust Him more than all your humanity and step forward into this predesigned warrior's super suit of faith—made just for you?

"Make them holy by your truth; teach them your word, which is truth. Just as you sent me into the world, I am sending them into the world. And I give myself as a holy sacrifice for them so they can be made holy by your truth. I am praying not only for these disciples but also for all who will ever believe in me through their message. I pray that they will all be one, just as you and I are one—as you are in me, Father, and I am in you. And may they be in us so that the world will believe you sent me."

John 17:17–21

Friend, Jesus has not only sent you but He, the Lord of all creation, is praying for you. The revival of your will to live solely for Him is not something that happens near you. It is an ignition within you. It is the combustion of God's love for you, through you—from Him, for Him.

When we honestly love God *more than all other things*, the outpouring of our life reflects the true heartbeat of revival. Because every revival is fueled from the same source—His love.

On this day, will you ask Him to ignite the unquenchable flame of His love within you? Will you invite the inferno of His presence to consume your heart, soul, mind and strength with the almighty power of His passion? Right now, will you ask for revival to awaken within you?

Precious Jesus,
I acknowledge that You have strategically placed me in this world to reach the lost with Your compassion.
Never was it Your will that I stay in the boat of Your love, speeding through this life and passing right by those who are dying in my midst.

Please open my eyes to see what You see—there are people in the water all around me!

Today, I choose to push through whatever ugliness might exist and pursue life! I choose to reach for them with the same tenacious love that You reached for me.

In this process, Jesus, help me to see the evil ropes of the enemy. I ask for Your wisdom to reach the hurting around me . . . without becoming entangled in the wreckage.

With all the strength You give me, I will draw them into the lifeboat of our Father's redeeming love.

Jesus, You are not sending me into the wreckage unprepared. I sense Your prayer for me—to finish here on earth what You started.

The revival of my will to live for God alone is not something that happens near me—but in me.

Father, I don't want to be lukewarm anymore. I don't want to live another minute outside of Your passion for this world, Your Great Commission. Right now, I avail all that I am—heart, soul, mind and strength—for You to set ablaze with unquenchable fire that burns for You alone.

Ignite my heart with such unrelenting heat that it blazes through every barrier of my unwillingness until there is nothing left—except a life consumed by Your compassion.

Jesus, I give this vessel for You to completely fill with Your love. May the light of Your presence flood into the darkness and become a beacon of hope. And may Your will be done here on earth as it is in heaven . . . through me.

I love You forever.
Amen.

Revival Rising

*Jesus, every revival starts the same way. Each
one is fueled by love—love for You alone.*

And Jesus came and said to them, "All authority in heaven
and on earth has been given to me. Go therefore and make
disciples of all nations, baptizing them in the name of the
Father and of the Son and of the Holy Spirit, teaching
them to observe all that I have commanded you. And
behold, I am with you always, to the end of the age."

Matthew 28:18–20 ESV

Friend, within your heart either Jesus is enough—or He is
not. What is your life proving you believe? Some of the
greatest threats of personal revival are pride and complacency.

We can become so prideful that it is easy to believe we are
"good enough" and do not need to follow Him any more than
we currently are. We can also become so complacent that genuine pursuit of our God is too much work, thereby becoming
content with old wine and small wineskins (see Mark 2:22). But
being content with old wine is the same as being content with
a droplet of Jesus' presence when an entire ocean awaits you.

In Psalm 34:8 we are encouraged to taste the Lord's goodness. Taste, consume, savor! Our God is calling us to experience every drop of the sea that is His glorious presence.

The revival of our hearts is not a spectator sport.

Jesus is our example (see Ephesians 5:1). He did not watch "the game" from heaven in His easy throne. He came down to earth and rushed onto the field of your heart and mine. He ran to finish first, competing as if our lives depended on Him completing the race—because they did. Jesus left behind the glory of heaven to defeat Satan on our behalf.

True redemption equals a true change of direction (see Luke 19:8–9). And the true change of direction we wish to see in the world begins one heart at a time, with our hearts first.

> And so dear brothers and sisters, I plead with you to give your bodies to God because of all he has done for you. Let them be a living and holy sacrifice—the kind he will find acceptable. This is truly the way to worship him.
>
> Romans 12:1

Indeed, our God continues to call those who are still listening.

It is time to leap forward into My perfect plan. It is time to fly into the realm for which you were created. I am sending you out into the blackness. I am sending you to earth . . . to transform it for My glory.

Beloved, it is time to leap into all you were created for.

Revival is reawakened within a *heart* when it chooses to:

- Embrace freedom by breaking the boomerang of the past
- Pursue God by getting in the truck of His presence
- See the unseen with the Father's love

Revival is restored within a *soul* when it chooses to:

- Trust that Jesus will never, ever let go
- Abide in faith and not be faithless any longer
- Engage worship to break off the enemy's attacks
- Pursue forgiveness by letting that junk go

Revival is renewed within a *mind* when it chooses to:

- Stop serving God with a spiritual flat and obey Him
- Allow belief to become breakthrough
- Radiate joy, the hallmark of the redeemed
- Pursue purity to see God's face

Revival is reinforced into *strength* when it chooses to lean into:

- Courage over being scared—which allows the enemy to win
- Standing firm, knowing that the enemy might start the fight, but Jesus always finishes it
- Genuine discernment, which begins with genuine listening

Revival is recharged when we fully understand the power of our testimony. It is released when we rely on inviting the Holy Spirit to lead intentionally. It is the relentless result when we choose to live for God alone and reach for those in the water while not getting entangled in the ropes of wreckage.

Revival begins when one chooses to be clothed with the very presence of the Lord Jesus Christ (see Romans 13:14).

Friend, within your heart, let today . . . be that day.

In this moment, Jesus, ignite all that I am—heart, soul, mind, strength—to burn for only You.

The world around me will not change—until I do. The transformation I seek begins with me. When I am fully consumed in the flame of Your presence, this is where revival will rise from my life.

Jesus, I ask for Your true redemption over my human religion. I release my humanity and ask for Your humility. I submit to the waterfall of Your transforming love to fill all that I am. Only then will the atmosphere around me be revived by the flood of Your redeeming passion through me.

May Your presence pour through me and raise a revival in my nation, my state, my county, my city, my neighborhood, my family and my home.

Your Word promises, "If my people who are called by my name will humble themselves and pray and seek my face and turn from their wicked ways, I will hear from heaven and will forgive their sins and restore their land" (2 Chronicles 7:14).

The ignition of my revival begins with bowing before You in humility, prayer, seeking, turning.

If I, this vessel, will persist in these four weapons of revival, then You will hear, forgive and heal the land of my heart, home and country.

I place my heart to be deeply united with Your heart in humility. I position my soul to be in constant communion with Your soul through prayer. I press into moving my mind into being pliable before Your mind to turn where You desire. I pursue with all the strength that is within me to seek You above all else.

Upon this bedrock, I lay myself in Your presence to be saturated with Your merciful healing—and forgiveness. From this foundation, I can be filled up and poured out for Your glory.

May I understand the power of Your complete redemption and wholeness working to create in me a unique weapon of loving warfare, ready to carry the light of my God into the darkness.

Today, I commit with all that I am to embrace the transforming fire that is Your presence.

Let Your revival rise in me.

Kim Meeder is the cofounder/CCO of Crystal Peaks Youth Ranch, a unique ministry that rescues mistreated horses and pairs them with hurting children, encouraging all toward the healing hope of Jesus Christ. The ranch was founded in 1995 and serves thousands of kids a year, all free of charge. Kim's first book, *Hope Rising*, was the inspiration for the ranch to win the national Jacqueline Kennedy Onassis Award and launched her international speaking ministry. She remains passionate to share *complete freedom* and wholeness in Christ by following the leadership of the Holy Spirit. Together, Kim and her husband, Troy, have helped to establish more than two hundred other similar ranch ministries throughout the United States and Canada, and a dozen in foreign nations. Kim and Troy have been married since 1981. They enjoy wilderness adventuring and live in Central Oregon.

More from Kim Meeder

The wild beauty of our God is calling, beckoning us to pursue Him beyond our circumstances, emotions and logic into the glorious mystery that is *Him*. Here are practical, everyday ways to pursue Him more passionately, to trust Him more fiercely, to see His face reflected in the miraculous and to experience His wild, limitless nature.

Encountering Our Wild God